THE INSIDER

GETTING
AN AGENT

THE INSIDER'S GUIDE TO
GETTING
AN AGENT

Lori Perkins

WRITER'S DIGEST BOOKS
CINCINNATI, OHIO

Other fine Writer's Digest Books are available from your local bookstore or direct from the publisher.

For information on more resources for writers visit our Web site at www.writersdigest.com.

To receive a free weekly newsletter delivering tips and updates about writing and Writer's Digest products, send an E-mail with "Subscribe Newsletter" in the body of the message to newsletter-request@ writersdigest.com or register directly at our Web site at www.writersdigest.com.

03   02   01   00   99   5   4   3   2   1

Library of Congress Cataloging-in-Publication Data

Perkins, Lori
   The insider's guide to getting an agent / by Lori Perkins.
     p.   cm.
  ISBN 0-89879-909-0 (alk. paper)
   1. Literary agents—United States. 2. Authors and publishers—United States. 3. Authorship—Marketing—United States. I. Title.
PN163.P47   1999
070.5'2—dc21   99-39515
                                                                CIP

Editor: David Borcherding
Designer: Angela Lennert Wilcox
Production editor: Bob Beckstead
Production coordinator: Rachel Vater

To my best friend and agent,

Peter Rubie

ACKNOWLEDGMENTS

There are so many people in publishing who taught me by their example. I very much believe in learning from others' mistakes, and I appreciate the honest feedback I received from so many editors, writers and agents.

I would not be the agent I am today if it were not for Patrick Filley, a vice president at Doubleday, who bought my first book in auction, and then proceeded to tell me to leave the sleazy agent I worked for and find an agency where my books spoke for themselves. Thank you for giving me the vote of confidence and the kick in the pants.

Dean Koontz shared an afternoon's worth of words of wisdom with me when I was a "baby" agent. (I asked him what I could learn about agenting from an established writer and he told me, honestly.) The war stories he shared with me have saved my clients a lot of money, and have always reminded me that I work for the writer, not vice versa. Thanks for taking the time with someone on the other side of the fence.

Eileen Fallon, with whom I have worked shoulder to shoulder on and off for the past fifteen years, has been a friend, a confidant, a co-worker and an inspiration. She was the one who told me not to be afraid of my strengths, even if they were in horror fiction and pop culture.

Thanks also to my authors, especially those who have stuck with me over these past fifteen years—Jeanne Cavelos, Chris Golden, Katherine Ramsland, Paul Sammon and Robert Weinberg, to name but a few. We have learned so much about this business, and ourselves, together. Thanks for making me part of your writing team. Thanks for listening to me when I was right, and thanks for having the strength to tell me when you thought I was wrong.

No book about writing would be complete without thanking the teacher who started the author on the right track, and this one is no exception. Thank you Arthur Feinberg, my sophomore English teacher at the Bronx High School of Science, who warned me not to make the same mistake he did. He said I shouldn't go into medicine, but should stick with words. He was right.

Thanks to my editors at Writer's Digest Books. Jack Heffron liked my voice and helped develop this book. David Borcherding read each chapter as it came out of the printer and forcefully encouraged me to meet my deadline.

ABOUT THE AUTHOR

Lori Perkins is the founding partner in Perkins, Rubie & Associates, a New York literary agency, where she represents some of the country's leading experts on frugality.

She is an adjunct professor at New York University where she teaches a class on Literary Agenting for N.Y.U.'s Center for Publishing.

Perkins is the author of *The Cheapskate's Guide to Entertaining: Fabulous Parties on a Modest Budget* (Carol Publishing), as well as *Finding the Agent Who's Right for You* (Writer's Digest Books).

She has contributed articles to *Writer's Market*, and a chapter on couponing for the frugality anthology, *The Simple Life* (Berkley).

Prior to becoming a literary agent, she was the publisher of *The Uptown Weekly News*, a weekly newspaper in Upper Manhattan.

Perkins has a B.A. from N.Y.U. in journalism and art history. She is a seasoned traveler and a frugality expert with a six-year-old son.

TABLE OF CONTENTS

EPILOGUE

Even Agents Need Agents . . . 199

APPENDICES

I have always written.

I wrote screenplays as a child. I wrote science fiction as a teenager. I finished my first novel in my free time in college, and when I graduated, I wrote for a living as a journalist.

I have always loved books. The only thing I'd rather be doing other than writing is reading.

I love the feel of books, the smell of books and the reflection of sunlight off book paper (both paperback and hardcover). I love the way books feel in my hands as I'm reading them, how they feel in my arms as I'm carrying them and how they weigh down my bag or knapsack as I'm walking somewhere. I hardly ever go anywhere without something to read.

I love libraries, bookstores and even the paperback racks of supermarkets. I always look at what books are on people's shelves when I go into their homes.

It's no wonder that I ended up working with people who write books. I've been a literary agent for more than fifteen years now, and I'm still thrilled when I sell a first novel or make a big sale for one of my clients. There is no bigger accomplishment than seeing one of the books that I have sold in a bookstore or in the hands of someone reading it on the subway.

I still love to write, too. Last year I sold my first book (with the help of my literary agent), and this is my second one. Writing books of my own has been a lifelong dream, and I can hardly find words to express how satisfied I feel about finally doing something I always knew I would.

I imagine that all of you reading this book are like me. You have always written. You've always known that some day you would write a book, and everything you've done until then has somehow been grist for the writing mill within you.

This is not a how-to-write book. I assume you already know how to do that. This is a how to get your book into the right hands and sell it book, so you can share your writing with all those who love to read.

This is a guerilla guide to getting published, a sort of no-holds-barred look at the inner workings of the publishing industry, a naked literary lunch. Once you've read this book and taken its advice to heart, you should be well on your way to getting an agent who can get you published.

This book will show you beyond a reasonable doubt that without a literary agent, you will not be published well. And, without the *right* literary agent, you will not continue to be well published. So finding the right literary agent for your work, career and personality is the second most important thing you can do in becoming a writer—after writing the book.

I want you to get published and to be well published, which is why I wrote this book.

I guarantee you that I would still be an unpublished writer if it were not for my agent. In addition to getting me multiple-book deals, reading my prose and giving me suggestions, guiding my career and making me face reality, he has made sure that my publishers and editors do the very best job they can with my books. From experience, I can tell you if I didn't have the right agent, you would not be reading this book.

PART I

THE BUSINESS

CHAPTER ONE

THE CHANGING PUBLISHING INDUSTRY

Or, Maxwell Perkins Is Dead and There Will Soon Be Only One Giant Publishing Company

When I began my career as a literary agent fifteen years ago, many of the old pros told me that they pitied me. They told me that it was too bad that I had started selling books in the mid-1980s, because it was just *so* hard to sell books nowadays. Back in the early 1970s, things were different, they said. They made me feel as though they were selling ten books a day way back in the ancient 1970s.

I hear this lament a lot now from other agents. It's so hard to sell books today, they say. The publishing industry has changed so much in the past decade, they moan.

Of course it has changed. Any industry that doesn't change with the times ceases to exist, and these have been rapidly changing times for both trends and technologies.

The biggest change in publishing in the past decade is the way books are now sold. This change affects all aspects of publishing, from the way books are marketed within the publishing house to how they are sold to the larger publishing industry, and finally to how they are sold to the public.

The way to truly appreciate these changes is to go back a bit to the way publishing used to be. Most aspiring writers know of the legendary editor Maxwell Perkins, who in his role as an editor at Scribner's nursed Thomas Wolfe, Ernest Hemingway, F. Scott Fitzgerald and countless other writers through writer's block, hangovers, bad relationships and periods of no advances. That was in the days when publishing was a "gentleman's profession," which means that highly educated (sometimes overeducated) individuals were paid meager wages (which they didn't mind because they had trust funds and inheritances to live off of) to find and publish literature, usually written by other overeducated gentlemen, which could be read by even more gentlemen. The concept of profit rarely figured into the purchasing of these books.

This all changed in the 1950s with the advent of mass market paperback books that could be read by everyone because they were small and affordable. This growth in popular literature went hand in hand with the popularity of television and the increasing upward mobility and education of the American public (especially through the G.I. Bill).

This popularization of reading as light entertainment as opposed to serious study led to the establishment of the fiction genres, which basically cover how books were sold in mass market. These seven basic novel categories haven't changed much in fifty years. You see books divided into these genres in most bookstores and libraries today. They are:

- Fantasy
- Horror
- Men's Action/Adventure (sometimes called Suspense or Thrillers)
- Mysteries
- Romance
- Science Fiction
- Westerns

The 1960s and the 1970s were the heyday of the mass market paperbacks, where, with the glorification of pop culture, even nonfiction reached readers in huge numbers. Nonfiction, too, began to be categorized, and you can see most of those subject areas in today's bookstores as well, with the emphasis on *Popular*. The categories that sprang up were:

- Biography (Frank Sinatra and Natalie Wood but not James Joyce)
- Business

- History/Current Affairs
- New Age (which used to be the Occult and/or Religion)
- Psychology (which covers everything from feminism to relationship books)
- Travel
- True Crime
- The instant book (which could be anything from *The Pentagon Papers* to a celebrity biography of a murdered star like Selena to the Olestra cookbook)

As the demographics of the readers of popular fiction changed with the times, growing younger and more female, so, too, did the demographics of the editors. The editorial staff changed from an almost entirely white male stronghold to an industry staffed mainly by women. In my opinion, this was because publishing salaries didn't rise with the times, so only educated, married women could afford to accept these meager wages, as they were still the second income in a two-income family.

"TRADE PUBLISHING" DEFINED

There are whole areas of publishing that haven't been mentioned, such as textbooks and children's books, but they are their own markets and are not as driven by popular taste and technology as what those in the publishing industry call *trade publishing*.

Trade publishing is a term you will hear repeatedly once you seriously decide to consider getting published, yet no one will offer to give you a definition of it. It is one of those terms that is thrown around by those in the know, and you are expected to understand it and to use it correctly or be labeled an outsider.

Trade publishing means any book that is sold through a bookstore. So trade publishing excludes self-published books (often referred to as *vanity press*), most religious books (which are sold through religious bookstores or by mail order), textbooks (which are sold through schools and university bookstores), and comic books and graphic novels, which are sold through comic book and hobby stores.

Now you may have noticed that some of the above kinds of books may make their way onto an occasional bookstore shelf (such as a popular self-published book on the history of a region or a graphic novel), but most people in the publishing industry still do not consider them *trade* books if they are not published by a *trade publisher*. Many people who work in the publishing industry act as if *trade publishing* is a synonym for what they consider to be "real" publishing, which to them means publication by a major New York publisher. Most of the nontrade publishing industry is located outside of New York, because it is just too expensive for publishers to do business from there.

VERTICAL PUBLISHING

Until the 1980s, most bookstores were privately owned Mom-and-Pop businesses, many of which specialized in certain kinds of books, such as mysteries or science fiction. Although most cities had a handful of large bookstores that were part of a regional chain, such as Barnes & Noble or Crown, there were no superstores or giant book cafes. In the 1990s, the chains started buying up the independent bookstores—or opening branches in malls and driving out the smaller stores. Bookselling became a much bigger business, and more books were sold, but it was more copies of the best-sellers, not a greater variety of titles.

The same thing was happening to publishing companies. On the heels of the paperback boom of the 1970s, paperback rights were suddenly going for hundreds of thousands of dollars because hundreds of thousands of copies were selling in the mass market. Bigger companies bought smaller companies, and then hardcover houses bought the paperback houses so that they would have an automatic outlet for their hardcover books in paperback (so they could publish a book "hard/soft," to use the publishing lingo). The number of paperback publishers went from twenty to eight within a decade.

When there were no more paperback companies to buy, the hardcover houses started merging. The smaller companies were being bought (and sometimes resold) to entertainment businesses and international conglomerates. This is when the concept of tying books to TV shows, movies and licensed products started to enter the publishing world. The West Coast accountants call this *synergy*. I just think it's a sin.

Publishing has gone from horizontal publishing to vertical publishing. Bertlesmann/Random House (whom we in the publishing industry now affectionately refer to as *Random Haus*) now encompasses seventeen publishers, including Anchor, Ballantine, Bantam, Broadway, Crown, Dell, Del Rey, Delacourt, Dial, Doubleday, Harmony, Fawcett, Knopf, Random House, Villard and Vintage. All of these companies were once independent publishers. Now they are all imprints.

There has been tremendous internal change within the individual publishing companies as a result of these mergers. For instance, in the summer of 1999, the reshuffling of the Bertlesmann/Random House deck began, with some companies from the old Bantam/Doubleday/Dell conglomerate combining with companies from the old Random House Publishing group to make new, smaller companies that may or may not survive in their present incarnation.

When I started selling books in 1985, there were twenty-three trade publishers to which to send a book. Now there are eleven, and some of my publishing peers would question my including some of these publishers as ''major'' publishers.

As the accountants and marketing consultants were brought in to look over the newly acquired publishing companies' lack of a predictable profit margin, they immediately discovered a solution—just publish more best-sellers. Books that had received small advances and sold 10,000 copies in hardcover or 50,000 copies in paperback were now too small for the publishing industry. Everyone was looking for first novels that could sell 100,000 copies. Authors and agents began lamenting the death of the *midlist book*, a phrase you hear at every publishing cocktail party.

A midlist book is a book that basically earns out its advance without changing the world. In hardcover, it sells between 8,000 and 15,000 copies; in trade it sells about 15,000 copies; and in mass market it sells between 25,000 and 50,000 copies. These books once paid the publishing bills one dollar at a time, but publishers have gotten greedy, looking for the breakout best-sellers that can pay for an entire season of publishing. They will only publish genre fiction and category nonfiction in the midlist range, which makes it harder and harder for a new author to break in.

THE EDITOR'S CHANGING ROLE

So instead of looking for good books, the publishing industry tried to manufacture surefire hits. Just as in the movie business, we now saw sequels (*The Lost World* and *Scarlett*), newly discovered trunk novels by dead authors (V.C. Andrews) and very little of anything really new. When I would ask editors what they were looking for, they would say last year's best-seller with a twist. When I started out in the business and would ask editors that same question, they answered "finely crafted fiction" or "good narrative nonfiction." Now we were basically hearing the buzzwords of Hollywood—*high concept* publishing.

Books were suddenly being "pitched" at editorial meetings. You'd hear outlandish phrases like "*Valley of the Dolls* meets *Dune*," and if it made sense to the people in marketing, who had been moved from the back office to the editorial table, the book would be bought. If the editor just said it was a well-written first novel that deserved to be published—forget it.

Meanwhile, things were growing more competitive in-house for editors. With the purchase of so many small companies, and so many editors in one conglomerate, there were semiannual bloodlettings—editors fired en masse, often during the summer or over the holiday season, when the industry slows down. Editors became more and more anxious to acquire "big" books and "big" authors, so their place would be secure.

Slowly, editors began to spend less time on the actual editing of books and more time cultivating contacts that would ensure that they were the ones in their publishing house who got first look at the big books from big agents. In some publishing houses, the editor's title has even changed to reflect this— they are now called *acquisitions* editors as opposed to *book* editors.

Editors also spent more time learning how to pitch books at editorial meetings to ensure that the books they brought up at editorial meetings got through. All of a sudden editors needed statistics and promotable authors with their own seminars and Oprah's private unlisted phone number, as opposed to just good books (although that still helps).

Editors were also being called upon to do more selling in-house. They pitched their books to the sales reps at sales conferences, which took place two to three times a year. They pitched their books to regional reps and booksellers. They pitched their books to foreign scouts (independent contractors hired by individual foreign publishers to look for big American books) and subsidiary rights departments (the people in-house who sell the foreign, audio, electronic, first serial, book club and other rights to a book). Essentially they spent most of their time selling their books to other people.

With all this acquiring and pitching, they had much less time to edit, so they started hiring more freelance editors, who were often their less marketing-savvy colleagues who had been fired the year before. Editors were now looking for more books in perfect condition, which they were willing to pay more for because they just didn't have the time to edit the way they used to.

One young editor was "caught" editing a manuscript at his desk by his publisher. When he was asked what he was doing and replied "editing," he was told he better discontinue the practice or he would lose his job. Needless to say, he left that publishing house and moved to another publisher where editors were still allowed to work on manuscripts. When that particular publisher was later fired, the editorial staff sang "Ding, Dong, the Witch Is Dead."

Because publishing companies were changing so radically, editors began moving from company to company much more rapidly than in the previous decade. Many editors became agents so that they could stay with writers longer and offer more editorial help. Other editors became "book doctors" and "editorial consultants."

To add to the confusion, two additional changes recently sideswiped the publishing industry—Amazon.com and wholesale clubs. No one in publishing predicted that so many people would be willing to buy books over the Internet or that so many copies of best-sellers would be bought at such deeply discounted prices. They were all too busy predicting the end of publishing as we know it because of the arrival of handheld computers that could download books and rid the world of paper forever.

The point that I'm trying to make with this very opinionated history of publishing is that the more things change, the more they stay the same. People will always say the sky is falling, but most of the time it's just rain, which actually helps things grow.

In spite of the fact that there are fewer publishers today than fifteen years ago, 10,000 more individual titles are published today than there were then. Who's reading, how they're buying and what they're buying will always change. It's up to the writer to reflect the times, and a good agent should know how and why those changes have taken place.

CHAPTER TWO

THE CHANGING ROLE OF THE AGENT IN PUBLISHING

Or, If Maxwell Perkins Were Alive Today, He'd Be an Agent

About ten years ago, when I was just a "toddler" agent, I attended a Manhattan writer's conference where a number of would-be authors asked the panel of esteemed editors and publishers where Maxwell Perkins was today? I remember a series of tortured answers from the editors attempting to explain how the economy of publishing had changed and how the book industry could no longer sustain that kind of nurturing commitment to writers.

I also remember the shocked expressions and Evil Eyes I received from those editors when I stood up in the audience and said that I believed that the spirit of Maxwell Perkins was alive and well in today's literary agents. The writers in the audience stood and clapped, and one of the editors said, "Oh, and I suppose you're a literary agent?"

Once upon a time, when a publishing company offered a contract to a writer, it was the personal relationship between the author and the editor that really sealed the deal.

The editor was expected to offer the writer detailed and wise criticism that would make the book stronger, and in so doing would teach the author new things about writing that would stay with him throughout his career. The editor took the writer to lunch frequently, offering him encouragement in the development of his next book. He was prepared to read chapters overnight as soon as they emerged from the typewriter. He would submit the writer's work for prizes and fellowships. He would extend deadlines if the work needed more time to reach its potential, often getting his publisher to dole out more money or a portion of the delivery and acceptance payment to keep the writer eating. In exchange for his loyalty, it was not unreasonable for a writer to expect to work with an editor for a decade or more and for an editor to feel anguish and loss should a writer even think about looking for greener pastures.

Those publishing days are over. Today, most editors don't stay at their houses long enough to warm their chairs (the average editor's tenureship seems to be about two years), most publishing companies have changed their corporate structure and name at least twice in the last decade, and only 1 percent of published writers make enough from writing to afford to make protein a regular part of their diet.

What's a writer to do? Get a good agent, of course. Where once agents were looked upon as a necessary evil, like lawyers and accountants, today it is virtually impossible to sell a book without an agent. Editors who buy fiction won't even look at a manuscript without representation, and many nonfiction editors will insist that you get an agent before they make an offer on a book. Needless to say, it is absolutely ridiculous to launch a career as a writer without an agent to guide you.

THE AGENT AS EDITOR

The description of what a good editor once did is now the definition of what a good agent can do. A writer once stayed with one editor, and consequently that editor's publisher, for his entire career. Today you'll find that same relationship is true of authors and their agents.

I've been an agent for fifteen years, and I have a number of clients who have worked with me for that entire time period. Not one of them has been published by the same publisher or editor consistently during that time. It is not because their editors no longer like their work or even because their books have not done well. It is because the publishing marketplace is so volatile.

Editors move from house to house like children playing musical chairs, changing not only employers, but even the kind of books they buy. One editor recently changed from buying humor to a position where she buys science books, and another went from editing a line of African-American romance novels to buying only nonfiction.

Publishers change what they are looking for each year, too. One year memoirs are the hot craze, the next it's Armageddon. Your agent, on the other hand, is always looking out for your best interests and will not be changing her clientele like bed sheets. In today's changing publishing world, the author/agent relationship is the most stable one.

When I was a "baby" agent, one of my clients had developed a strong bond with his editor (I had too—it was my first sale). She took a long time to make him an offer on his second book, which was richer and more nuanced than his first. Even though the first novel had received strong reviews and had sold to paperback, her offer was only slightly larger than that for the first novel, and I was certain that this novel would be worth more than what she had offered if I were to place it on the open market. I begged my author to let me show his material to a few editors who had expressed interest in his work.

I explained to my author that it wasn't so much that I wanted to move the book (I liked his publisher and editor), but that I wanted to get him more money for it so that the publisher would treat it with more respect. I didn't want him to be plagued by the *Second Novel Syndrome*, in which the sophomore book is sent out into the marketplace to fend for itself, unhyped and alone.

His editor got wind of my desire to test the market and begged him to accept her offer. She reminded him of how she had discovered him and how much she loved his work. He fell for it and told me to accept her offer. I did because Dean Koontz once offered me the advice that the one thing I should always remember as an agent is that I work for the writer, not the other way around. He reminded me that it isn't *my* writing career, but my author's.

Needless to say, a week later this editor called me with the good news that she had accepted a senior editor position at another publishing house. My author had been "orphaned," a practice so common in publishing today that many authors have never had the same editor from the time of acquisition through publication. Some authors have even had three or four editors during the two years it usually takes to go from signing a contract to publishing a book.

A good, well-respected agent can save your book from oblivion. Like a superhero, she can come in and rescue your book from a bad (or just plain bored) editor, get the book reassigned to someone who is right for you or, if absolute worst should come to worst, move the book to another house and pay back the advance—without having your writing career go down in flames. Without someone who knows the pitfalls and minefields of publishing, an orphaned book can die, killing the author's career at the same time. (I can't tell you the number of times I've had editors look up an author's sales record and ask if he would consider *changing his name* so that they could publish the new book as a first novel, after disastrous sales on earlier books.)

The role of the agent in publishing has changed so dramatically over the past twenty years that editors and writers often don't recognize us anymore. Where once we were mere business managers, today we are truly author's representatives, expected to give advice on everything from plotting to publicity.

When I started in this business fifteen years ago, there were about 500 agents on both the East and West coasts, concentrated mainly in the large, established agencies such as William Morris and International Creative Artists. Today, there are twice as many agents. Our ranks have been filled by the changes in publishing—namely by editors who have left publishing to become agents. About half the literary agents working today are former book editors, and of those who have become agents recently, nearly all have come to this side of the business as a result of publishing mergers. In my office alone, my business partner and my two agent colleagues (with whom I share office space) are all former book editors.

With so many former book editors working as literary agents, it should be no surprise that editors are relying on agents more heavily for clean, well-edited books. They know they don't have to do that work themselves anymore (and they don't really have the time, with all the in-house selling they have to do), and they know they can trust our judgment.

I have line-edited and/or replotted just about all the books of the first-time authors I've worked with, and I've enjoyed doing the work. There's a bonding process that takes place between the author and his first "editor." In today's publishing world, that editor is more often than not the literary agent.

THE AGENT AS MARKETER

In addition to knowing how to edit, a literary agent who has worked for a publisher also knows the inner workings of how a book is acquired. She knows what the marketing department wants to hear in a proposal and how to juggle the figures to make the profit and loss statement work. (Also known as the *P&L*, this statement is the result of an editor guesstimating a book's projected revenue—guessing how many copies of a book have to sell at a certain price before the book earns money.) She knows where the booby traps are in publishing contracts and how to sweet talk the contracts department into giving the client some slack on publishing clauses.

Once the manuscript has been delivered, an agent will either begin selling the subrights herself, bringing the author additional revenue from magazine, movie and foreign sales, or motivate the publisher's subrights department into getting a jumpstart on sales. She also knows how to get the most from publicity (and when to tell the author to step in and do something on his own). But most of all, what an agent who has worked for a publisher can do is guide the author through the maze that is publishing and let him know what to realistically expect.

When I talk to editors and writers about how I see the role

of the agent as becoming more editorial and more essential to the author's success, they often ask me why I didn't become an editor. At the beginning of my career, I wondered this myself. After all, I had been trained as a newspaper editor. I quickly learned, however, that the added bonus of being an agent, rather than an editor, is that I get as many chances as I want to get something I believe in published. My poor editor colleagues get only one shot. If the marketing department turns them down or they lose the book to another editor, that's usually it.

In all fairness to the best editors out there, I do have one story about an editor who believed in a book almost as much as I did. He tried to buy a book while working at one company, got another job a year later, and then called me with an offer on Christmas Eve because he knew I had not yet sold the book. The book has gone on to make more than $50,000 in royalties and has sold in five countries.

I have sold a novel that was rejected by thirty-three editors (it took me two-and-a-half years to sell). I have sold oddball projects that I was told were impossible to sell (a coffeetable art book about *The Twilight Zone* that took me four years to straighten out the permissions for, and then the first publisher I sold it to told me to find another publisher because the printing costs had gone up and they couldn't afford to publish it the way the author envisioned it) because I believed in the books—and I believed in my ability to sell them.

Although the publishing industry continues to change, I still stand by the belief I stated to that writer's conference a decade ago: The spirit of Maxwell Perkins remains alive in today's literary agents.

CHAPTER THREE

DIFFERENT KINDS OF AGENTS:

Editors, Lawyers and Salespeople

To the unpublished, the world of books often looks monolithic. When I attend writer's conferences, there are always a handful of writers who are surprised that editors really do specialize in certain types of books, as do agents. They think all people who work with books must have the same skills, and that we are all created equal.

I used to think this way, too. Before I worked in publishing, I thought there was one basic secret to publishing well, and that all the successful editors and agents knew what it was. And there is. It's just different for each editor and agent, and for each writer, too.

Here it is: Find one thing you do better than anyone else you know and work on it until you are the absolute best at it that you can be. Then be proud of your ability to do it.

It took me a while to really live this motto. I came into book publishing from the back end, having worked five years as a newspaper publisher and editor. I assumed that what I would sell well as an agent would be books by journalists, because I had been one and because I knew so many. But a crucial detail that I overlooked was that I wasn't an investigative reporter, but a feature writer. The newspaper I founded was really a feature paper because it came out every other week. I filled it with entertainment stories, such as interviews with celebrities who had grown up in Washington Heights or articles about the architectural history of the neighborhood. Even the news stories were soft news.

Hard news is much more respected than feature writing by the news business and those that give out awards (think *Time* vs. *People* or People's Choice vs. Pulitzer Prize), so I ignored my innate talent and abilities and tried to sell current affairs books—but it was hard going.

However, whenever I had a book about TV or art or music, I could sell it in a snap. One day I realized I was really good at selling pop culture, so I decided to specialize in it. I could sell highbrow pop culture (anything from literary biographies of Anne Rice and Dean Koontz to surrealistic interpretations of the art of *The Twilight Zone*) to lowbrow (a Kirk Cameron biography that sold 200,000 copies and the first *Brady Bunch* book.) Editors started calling me when they had complicated pop culture ideas. "We want an upscale *Star Wars* tie-in," one editor told me, so I sold him *The Science of Star Wars* by a former astrophysicist and NASA scientist—and everyone was thrilled. When I looked at my clientele more carefully, I saw that I did represent a lot of journalists, but that they all came from the feature pages.

The same thing happened to me with fiction. Because I had grown up in New York City and had connections to a major New York university's writing program as well as the various writing workshops throughout the city, I assumed that I would represent *literary* fiction. I think everyone who enters publishing has pretentious aspirations of finding the next great American novelist, but again, I really wasn't reading many of them. When people asked me what I was reading, I lied and said the latest Roth or Updike, but in truth I usually had a King or a Koontz or a Rice in my shoulder bag.

There was another agent in my office who made a good living selling romance novels. Editors told me she was one of the best in the romance business, and they said it with respect and a little bit of awe. I could tell that she really loved the material she sold (she took the day off to watch the royal wedding). She was also known for her ability to guide her authors to bigger and better things, and they stayed with her for years. She was the one who told me to find my niche in publishing, and it was the best advice I ever received.

At about the same time, there was a boom in horror fiction. First horror novels were suddenly selling by themselves. We had weekly editorial meetings in the agency I worked at, and one afternoon my boss asked if any of us had read anything by this guy Stephen King. I shyly admitted that I had actually read every single one of his novels, plus his short story collections, and she said, "Good. You're now the horror agent."

In one week, I sold four horror first novels, where it had taken me nearly a year to sell the two literary novels I had labored over. And I'd made a lot more in commissions from the sale of the horror novels than the literary fiction. I had been liberated. There was no turning back.

While I know how to edit (I have a degree in it) and I believe I know how to write, what I do best is sell. And when I finally knew what I should sell (which was simply what I was well read in and had a passion for), I became a very good and confident agent.

Just as it took me a while to learn what I should sell, it took me some time to accept that I was better at pitching than editing or even writing. When I ran my newspaper, I couldn't afford to pay my reporters what I really thought their stories were worth, so I would always suggest that they call so-and-so at such-and-such a magazine or newspaper (whom I had gone to college with or knew from the newspaper grapevine) so they could earn some extra money for the work they had done for me. One day one of my reporters said, "You know, you should be an agent. You're always telling us who to send our stuff to and what angle we should pitch." And he was right.

I found it was much easier to sell other people's work than my own because I never felt self-conscious about saying the work was good or commercial or worth more than what they were offering. I found that if I truly believed in something, I could be a tenacious advocate.

Becoming an agent was the perfect job for me. It brought together the best of my skills, which were a love of reading, editing and selling. I'd learned to sell as the newspaper's publisher, pounding the pavement days before the printer needed to be paid and getting the local banks to give us ads. My advertising manager would ask me how I did it, and I'd always say I believed in the paper and the printer's threat that he wouldn't print the next edition if I didn't pay for the last one.

When I became an agent, I discovered that most agents had come to the job from some long and winding road that had something to do with words, just as I had. No one had gone to college thinking they would grow up to be a literary agent.

I have found that agents tend to come from three areas of professional ability: In their previous lives, they were either editors, lawyers or salespeople.

IN A FORMER LIFE . . .

As I said previously, more than half the agents working today were once book editors. If you add in the agents who were newspaper or magazine editors, the percentage of agents with editorial experience is close to 65 percent.

The next largest professional background includes those with legal experience. Many former lawyers came from the entertainment side of law and found that they preferred working for writers rather than publishers and studios. Many of these former lawyers have also put in a stint or two in Hollywood, where they've also tried their hands at being producers or talent agents. People who have worked in a publisher's contracts department also fall into this category, which I'd say makes up about 20 percent of the agenting business.

About 15 percent of literary agents have been flat out salesmen, selling everything from cars to stocks to advertising. One agent I know used to sell vacuum cleaners door to door. People who have put in a year or two selling subsidiary rights for publishers also fall into this category.

I am now teaching a class on agenting at New York University's Center for Publishing. It's a night school for college graduates who are interested in careers in publishing. I was surprised that the work backgrounds of the students in my class seemed to mirror the above percentages.

WHICH IS BEST?

When I speak at writer's conferences and tell audiences of unpublished authors that they will have to decide what kind of agent they want, someone usually raises a hand and says, "I want any kind I can get." This is often followed by a sad story about how hard it is to get an agent.

I know that's true, but if you're serious about becoming a published writer, you will need an agent—and you will need to know what you can expect from your agent. Otherwise, you will be disappointed and angry and could sabotage your own career before it gets off the ground.

Most previously unpublished book authors need an editorial agent at the beginning of their career because they have never written a full-length book. What they don't know is that they will need advice and handholding in every area of the writing process, from how to work and write at the same time to dealing with an editor's editorial suggestions. Most first-time authors are shocked at how hard it is to write (and rewrite) that first book.

However, a handful of writers just don't want editorial suggestions from anyone but an editor (and some don't even want their editor's advice). They don't want to rewrite a book for an agent on "spec." These writers should work with agents who have stronger sales backgrounds.

Authors with track records, and celebrity authors, often feel that the publishing offers they receive for their books came to them because of who they are. They believe that the actual deal-making and contract language is the area where they can get the best terms from a publisher and often hire a literary agent with a legal background.

Some extremely successful authors, such as Stephen King, once started with a traditional literary agent, but after years of best-sellerdom have opted to hire a lawyer with a literary practice who just charges (heftily) by the hour instead of taking a commission on the entire earnings of the book.

The other thing a writer should think about before choosing an agent is whether he wants to be a big fish in a little pond or a guppy in a great lake. What I mean by this is, if you want an agent who will read your work quickly, give you feedback and brainstorming sessions and work with you, you probably want to be represented by a smaller agency.

Although it may be an ego boost to be represented by the same agency as Thomas Harris and Whoopi Goldberg, a new or unpublished author rarely gets the same care as a celebrity or successful author. If you are represented by a large agency, you will have to get in line to get your agent's attention. However, the benefit of a bigger agency is that when an agent calls an editor, the editor return his calls right away, because he's hoping to get a crack at the next Seinfeld book. A smaller agency (or independent agent) is known by the books they've sold but is unknown to an editor who has never done business with them before.

If you know the basic types of agents out there and what you want, the next step is for you to find out exactly what kind of books each agent sells and match your writing to the perfect agent for your book.

CHAPTER FOUR

WHAT DO LITERARY AGENTS REALLY DO?

The Not-So-Glamorous World of Those Whom Lunch Revealed

Before I became a literary agent, I used to think that New York literary agents were mystical beings who would change my life with one phone call, if they would only respond to my query letters. When I finally left the news business and became a literary agent, I was honestly surprised to find that agents are mere mortals with no super powers, only high-powered Rolodexes and a nearly insane desire to get people published.

Now that I'm on the other side, I know that a literary agent with a good reputation receives at least a thousand query letters a month. Is it any wonder that my early requests for representation went unanswered or were answered months later with those obnoxious mass-produced form letters?

Looking back, I realize that I had no idea what literary agents really did. I imagined that they came into work and read query letters every day, just waiting for that brilliant manuscript (which, of course, was written by me) to land on their desks and change their lives (and mine). I imagined they spent hours talking to their other brilliant clients about how brilliant their work was and then spent the rest of the day talking to editors about how brilliant everything they represented was.

Editors, of course, knew how brilliant the agents were, so they interrupted the editing of other brilliant writers' manuscripts to take these agents' calls. When the brilliant manuscripts that the agents told them about arrived on their desks, they read them overnight and immediately went into their publishers' offices the next morning to ask for as much money as they could get for these masterpieces.

I also knew that the publishing lunch was some mystical literary alchemy experience, much like joining a secret society. Once you were a member of this literary fraternity of editors, agents and writers who swore their blood oaths over lunch at New York's best restaurants, you were in for life.

I had gleaned this fantasy about agents and editors and the publishing industry from all the movies I'd seen (*Misery* and *Romancing the Stone* are two that come to mind) and all the articles I'd read about the glamorous world of publishing in such diverse places as *USA Today* and *The New Yorker*.

These fantasies had a modicum of truth to them (agents, editors and writers do a lot of business over lunch, but it's hard work, not magic). They had been so embellished in my imagination that reality was hard to take.

I know, too, that because of these Hollywood depictions of book agents, writers often have unrealistic expectations of what an agent can do. Some writers expect me to be their editor, business manager, lawyer, publicist, banker, therapist, groupie, mother, new best friend or fairy godmother.

A synonym for agent is *author's representative*, and that really is a perfect definition of the agent's role. An agent is your representative to the publishing industry, who you hire to negotiate in your best interests.

Robert Weinberg, an author whom I've represented for my entire agenthood, told a group of fellow horror writers that an agent should be like "a good Jewish mother." He explained this by adding, "As per the movies and real life—pushy, annoying, constantly questioning, and wanting the very best for you. I know that not everyone likes this type of personality—and many people can't stand it. But having had a Jewish mother, I can testify to the results."

A BIT OF REALITY

A little bit of reality can go a long way in preparing you for a long and successful relationship with an agent. You need to know what to realistically expect.

What an agent does can vary slightly from agent to agent,

but it generally falls into the following basic tasks (assuming your material is ready for submission):

- Knowing who to send your work to
- Helping you choose the right publisher/editor (should more than one be interested)
- Negotiating the terms of your contract
- Representing the foreign and subsidiary rights to your book (film, magazine, audio, electronic, etc.)
- Making sure that your publisher keeps you informed of your book's progress before and after publication
- Preparing your next project for submission and negotiating those terms
- Keeping on top of the financial and legal aspects of your books after publication
- Giving you career guidance, for both the long and short term, along the way

Most of all, what you need to remember is that agents are human. We have no incantations to force editors to buy your books (none of us have made any deals with the devil that I know of). We just have our word and reputation and the weird belief that good writing should be published.

When I go to writer's conferences, authors are always amazed that I don't read manuscripts in the office and that I read at the same speed they do. One author actually thought I had some special ability to read manuscripts at superhuman speed.

My first job as an agent was as an assistant agent to a sleazy New York agent who desperately wanted to go Hollywood by attaching himself to book projects as a producer. He was every writer's nightmare of what a bad agent could be. He charged authors for manuscript evaluations (which he never did himself), he used his clients for their contacts, and he had the lowest ethical standards imaginable.

I worked for him for only six months, and even that was too long, but he did teach me the basics of the business. I sold two books in four months, one of which went into auction, and everyone I knew in publishing told me that I was a natural agent.

Even this poor excuse for an agent never had time to read manuscripts in the office. He was on the phone to editors and his authors from the minute he got in until he left. I read the manuscripts for him, which was fortunate for those writers who sought him out at that time because I had more of a literary background than he did. When I left his agency, I took eleven clients with me—all of whom were previously unpublished—and I managed to sell a book for every one of them.

However, most of the people who act as the first screening level in an agent's office are young and do not have much editorial experience. They are instructed to reject at least 90 percent of the material that comes into the office. But they are usually eager to find new talent, as I was, and may one day grow into agents or editors themselves.

Editorial assistants and assistant agents are your link to the future. If you are an unpublished writer, you should be looking to find a literary soulmate in an up-and-coming assistant (I'll tell you how to do this in chapter six).

It is very rare for an established agent to take on a writer from unsolicited manuscripts, which those in publishing affectionately call *the slush pile* (or just *slush*) or the "unsoliciteds." This happens so rarely nowadays that when it does, it makes the news (although I've done it once or twice this year, but that's out of a thousand query letters). However, my first year as an agent, I sold fourteen first novels, all of which were cultivated from the slush pile, so you can see how the odds stack up.

WHY GET AN AGENT?

What agents do in the office is talk on the phone, mostly to editors. They pitch the books they are currently trying to sell, follow up on submissions they've already made, negotiate terms for books that an editor has made an offer on and guide their clients through the shaping process in putting together their next book.

They also oversee a vast assortment of assistants who copy, collate and staple (and sometimes mutilate) the material that they've pitched to the editors, as well as give reader's reports on manuscripts and cull through the slush.

It takes about two weeks to get a response on the average nonfiction proposal. I hope to hear from editors of fiction within a month, but it often takes longer because it's a holiday season, the editor isn't really looking for new fiction or the market is tight. I spend a lot of time following up on my submissions, since I usually have twenty projects on submission at one time.

I negotiate contracts, too, making sure there are no onerous clauses that entitle the publisher to the writer's first book, and firstborn child as well. I also chase down writers' payments. Although an assistant can do this, I find it is more effective if the agent does it herself.

You may now be saying to youself: That's all very nice, but do I really need an agent? Couldn't I do all that myself? Look at the list of things an agent does and tell me you have the time, ability and inclination to handle it all without making mistakes that could set back your career in ways you can't even imagine. Let me put it to you another way: Only a fool has himself for a client.

That's not to say that authors haven't sold a book or two themselves, but there's much more to being an agent than making a sale.

One writer came limping to our firm after selling a book himself. He had had a falling out with his agent years ago and decided to handle his own deal this time around. When his contacts didn't pan out as well as he had hoped, he sold *all* rights to his novel (including foreign and film) for $1,000, and similar rights to the next work, because he was so relieved to finally have a publisher. It was only after the paperback, foreign and made-for-TV movie deals were made and he received only a fraction of the money that he realized he'd screwed himself. He begged us to break his contract, and we managed to save him from this publishing purgatory.

Often when an author sells his own book, a good editor will refer him to an agent to guide him through the contract and production process and fill him in on all the publishing details that the editor doesn't have the time to explain. Editors edit.

Agents know what the industry norms are (such as how much the industry is paying right now for certain kinds of books, what rights are selling and where a house is flexible on contract terms). They know the history of the publisher with your kind of book, as well as the strengths and weaknesses of your editor and the industry gossip on which publishing houses are up for sale.

And agents have clout. When your publisher (and editor) does a deal with your agent, the entire agency roster is on your side. They don't want to upset your agent because it might affect another book they have under contract or their chances of getting one of your agent's really hot writers when their next book comes up.

But that's not the only reason you need an agent. When I entered the publishing business, I was stunned at the sheer number of books published every year (about 65,000 in 1997). Only someone who eats (we lunch professionally), sleeps and schmoozes books for a living could possibly keep up with who's buying what for how much and why. Writers write. If you're spending the amount of time necessary to keep up with the publishing business, you are either working for *Publisher's Weekly* or not as serious about writing as you should be.

A DAY IN THE LIFE

The best way to tell you what agents really do is to describe a typical work day. I start at 10:00 A.M. because editors straggle into their offices late, and I work until 6:00 P.M. The first thing I do is call all the editors who have promised to respond to me by that day and to check up on projects on submission. Most of the time I leave a message, and the editors get back to me after lunch.

I then prepare the day's multiple submissions, which includes writing pitch letters, calling all the editors and pitching the book, and then getting everything packaged by 5:00 P.M. for UPS.

Lunch is an extremely important part of my business. It's where I get to know individual editors' taste, learn what they and their publishing houses are buying right now, hear industry gossip and pitch my agency for future projects. A good, productive lunch can net me up to ten book sales over a year. I rarely remember what I've eaten, but I always remember what the editor is interested in. (How else would I know that the head of Harper's science fiction line is a sometimes gardener, so if I ever have a book on science fiction plants, he's my editor?)

Lunch is therefore sacred, and I do it seriously. I usually have lunch at 12:30 P.M., which means I leave my office at noon to travel. Lunch lasts about two hours, and I'm always back at my desk by 3:00 P.M. I tell you this because you should never call an agent between noon and 3:00 P.M. Eastern Standard time, unless you just want to leave a message. As agents, we should be out to lunch, and if we are in our office answering phone calls, we're not doing our job.

I keep a sixteen-page client list that describes the past and present work of all the agency's authors. I give this to every editor I have lunch with, and I tell them to look it over carefully when they get back to the office and to let me know if there are clients or titles that interest them. I suggest they make copies and share it with other editors. This client list is a very valuable calling card, but one I only give out face to face. I cannot tell you the number of deals that have come about as a result of leaving this list with editors.

During the afternoon, I call back editors who have returned my calls, go through the mail and perhaps read over a contract or prepare a foreign mailing (I have eleven foreign agents who represent my books throughout the world, and I send them monthly bulletins about my books along with a mailing).

From 5:00 P.M. to 6:00 P.M. I call my authors, because I don't have to worry about being interrupted by editors—their work day is over. I can devote my full attention to my authors this way. I also return phone calls from the West Coast at this time, because they are just returning from their lunches.

I get home, have dinner, put my son to sleep, unwind, and then try to read at least an hour each weeknight and five hours over the weekend. I average about one novel and four or five proposals a week.

I represent about fifty writers, each of whom writes at least one book a year. Some write as many as four, and I have one author who wrote ten books this year, but he's an exception. My stable of writers pretty much takes up my reading time. The same is true of my partner, Peter Rubie, although he reads more of the unsolicited query letters we receive than I do.

Most agents represent between fifty and seventy-five writers. If an agent is established, she is quite busy with the authors she has already made a commitment to and will relegate responding to query letters as a lesser priority. As I mentioned, most agents assign this task to the lowliest person in the office, or wait until the pile is so high you can cut through it only with a scythe.

Right now we receive about 1,000 query letters a month, so it takes a while to respond to all the mail. We have hired a college English student whose job it is to sift through our unsolicited mail and call our attention to those letters that fit our tastes. She's very good at it. My partner and I then read through this material when we have a free moment, which is very rare. This is why it often takes up to three months to get a form rejection letter in your self-addressed stamped envelope (SASE). This is also why it's so important for you to include that SASE in your mailing.

Just as the publishing market changes, a good agent changes her tastes and skills with the market. Although I represent both fiction and nonfiction, nearly all of the agency's clients have been, or still are, journalists. So when one market declines, we often move a client into another area of that market (from adult to young adult fiction or to nonfiction) while their

> This book is the perfect example of the difference a good agent can make to a writer's success. I had written a book proposal that the editor liked but could not get his publisher to buy. He came back to my agent apologetically, saying he'd like to work with me on something else. My agent made a few suggestions (knowing my interests and abilities), and when my editor said he wanted to see a proposal on one of them, I quickly responded. We had an offer within weeks.

genre is in a slump, so they can continue to publish (and pay their mortgages).

Because my partner and I were both journalists before we became agents, we can also come up with ideas for our clients when their own ideas don't sell. We've received quite a reputation for coming up with book ideas from editors, and now editors often call us with books that they're looking for. We represent the author, not just the book. About a third of our business is now done this way.

Some literary agencies have agency contracts, but I do not. When I sell a book, the publishing contract includes a clause that ensures that I am the agent of record for that title until the rights revert. That's all I need.

When I was an apprentice agent at another agency, I worked under someone who insisted on contracts for all her writers. She wanted a piece of all their work during the time she represented them (such as articles they sold themselves), as well as a piece of the option book, even if she didn't sell it. The one thing her writer's contract taught me was that an unfair contract can always be broken.

Working for that firm also taught me that there was no way to hold on to a writer who wanted to leave, and that I didn't want to represent anyone who didn't want me to represent them.

Most agents today take a 15 percent commission on domestic sales and 20 percent on foreign sales (because they split

---

AGENCY CLAUSE

The Author hereby confirms that s/he has irrevocably appointed and designated **Perkins, Rubie Associates** (hereafter referred to as the "Agent") of 240 West 35 Street, Suite 500, New York, NY 10001 as the Author's sole Agent throughout the world with respect to the Work and all rights herein. The Author hereby authorizes and directs the Publisher to pay and forward all statements and monies accruing from the Publisher to the Agent, and the Publisher agrees to do so. The Author hereby empowers the Agent to act on the Author's behalf in all matters arising from or pertaining to this Agreement and/or the Work. The Author hereby irrevocably agrees to pay the Agent, and the Author hereby irrevocably authorizes the Agent to receive and retain, and the Author hereby irrevocably assigns and transfers to the Agent an amount equal to fifteen percent (15%) of all monies accruing, payable or paid to the Author under this Agreement and otherwise accruing from the Publisher or Author with respect to the Work, and the Publisher hereby accepts and agrees to honor said assignment and transfer. Any sum payable by the Publisher under this Agreement and paid to the Agent pursuant to this paragraph shall constitute a valid discharge of the Publisher with respect thereto. The Author warrants that he has secured the rights to the Work and that he has given the Agent clearance to represent him on the Author's behalf. The Author indeminifies the Agent and holds them harmless from any legal action that may result from the contents or presentation of the books.

I've included our agency clause, which we insert into every contract we negotiate. This agency clause acts as an agency agreement for books that we have sold. We feel this clause covers all the bases for both the author and the agent.

this with foreign agents). The older (established prior to 1975) and bigger agencies take a 10 percent commission, because they have the estates of long-dead writers to fill their coffers without worrying about new sales. Some agencies charge for expenses such as phone calls, faxes and postage and most also charge for copying.

AGENCY LETTER OF AGREEMENT

February 11, 1999

Dear _____,

As requested, please regard this letter as a declaration of a business relationship between yourself and **Perkins, Rubie Associates**.

I agree to take you on as a client of **Perkins, Rubie Associates** and will make my best efforts to guide you and enthusiastically represent your work in the publishing and related industries both in North America and abroad through our foreign agents; should you so desire I will also put forth my best efforts to get you representation with our motion picture and television associates.

For my efforts, we will take 15% (fifteen percent) of any monies earned, which shall be written into any publishing contract we are successful in making on your behalf. A commission for any movie or TV deals we are successful in making for you with a Hollywood co-agent will be split 50/50 between the co-agent and ourselves. Foreign sales will be charged at 20% (10% for the foreign agent and 10% for **Perkins, Rubie Associates**).

Either party is free to notify the other that they wish to terminate this agreement, as long as it is done in writing and with one month's notice.

Best Regards,

Peter Rubie

This is a sample letter we send out when a client requests a formal letter of agreement with the agency.

Just as I use foreign agents to sell my client's books in foreign countries, I use West Coast agents to sell my author's books in Hollywood. I find that since the studios are in Los

Angeles, you have to be out there to make those sales, just as you have to be on the East Coast to sell books.

I have relationships with seven different Hollywood agents, each of whom has a success rate and liking for different areas of my list, such as young adult fiction or true crime. I learned to use different film agents when I tried to pressure one of my Hollywood agents, who had sold two of my projects, into taking on a third. He told me that it just didn't ring his bells, and I sort of said, "So what?" He told me that representing my entire list of clients was like asking me to represent an entire extended family of writers. There was no guarantee that I would like their work just because they were all related. That made sense to me, and I vowed to match my writers with Hollywood agents who had the same passion for their work as I did.

Is this the glamorous life you imagined I led? I doubt it. Most of my interns and assistants are shocked at the amount of paperwork in this business and how little free time there is (especially when you realize that I work straight through lunch, so I don't even have time to fill a prescription or window shop during the lunch hour).

But I love what I do, and there have been glamorous moments in my career. For me, they included meeting two of my adolescent writing idols—Dean Koontz and Anne Rice—going to London for a writer's conference (most of them are in much less exciting places) or the time I sold a book my boss double-dared me not to take on for $110,000 in a two-day auction with seven bidders.

Ultimately, the glamour of the business is in the work itself.

CHAPTER FIVE

THE BUSINESS BEHIND PUBLISHING LUNCHES

Where the Deals Happen

Although there are many elements to being an agent other than schmoozing, the essential task of agenting is matchmaking between editors and authors, with the agent as the go-between. For this reason, when you distill all that agents do, the editorial lunch is still one of the most important, and yet mystical, parts of being an agent. It is where a great deal of our business really takes place.

I've had many lunches where I've walked away from the table knowing that I would continue to do business with that editor and had probably earned thousands of dollars in commission in one two-hour meeting. Other lunches were so awkward that I knew I would never submit another book to that editor again.

No one taught me how to have an editorial lunch. I was just thrown to the lions when I was sent to meet a young editor for a "drinks date" (which is what editorial assistants and junior agents go on, because they have to be in the office to answer the phone while the big cheeses are out to lunch). However, I quickly learned that there's a pattern to these get-togethers; essential information must be shared, or the lunch is a waste of time for both of us.

For a lunch with an editor I've never met before, my objective is to get a feel for her tastes and what she has been told to buy by her publishing board. Sometimes I know a little bit about the editor before we meet face to face, because I've submitted something to her (usually as a result of a referral from another editor or agent). However, sometimes I know next to nothing about her tastes because she's replaced another editor who bought one of my books (see Orphaned Books in chapter eighteen) or she's called me out of the blue because another editor I know has said we should meet.

When meeting with us for the first time, most editors' goals are to find out what our bigger books are and to get us to promise to let them be the person at their conglomerate who sees the next big book first. In today's publishing world, getting first look at something really hot can make or break an editorial career, so the agent/editor contacts are more important to the successful editor than they were in the past. Sometimes editors use the lunch as a brainstorming session because they know we represent a certain type of client (a science writer, for instance). Sometimes they just want us to know that they're interested in stealing a certain client.

THE RULES

In the rules of the agent/editor game, it is the editor who usually picks the restaurant and the time of the lunch. Some agents feel that having the upper hand in even this small a decision sets the tone for the business dealings, and they will actually negotiate the location (deciding who has to travel) and the time.

The same agents who negotiate every detail of the where and when of the lunch also have a pecking order for who should arrive first and how long they should wait. Unless either one of us is traveling a great distance, we really try to arrive on time, especially since editors usually have meetings to go to in the afternoon.

Editors will usually bring a company catalog, and perhaps one or two books that they've edited, to give the agent an overview of what they're buying. I will bring a copy of our client list, which is a twenty-page list of the authors we represent, detailing their present projects as well their publishing history. The client list is like an agency catalog, except we organize it by author, not by book.

The food is the least important part of the lunch. When I first started in the business (and I was considerably younger and burning up calories at a much faster rate), I was much more interested in the variety of fabulous restaurants we went to, but after years and years of cous cous, grilled tuna and risotto, the meals have all run together and it is the conversations and contacts that stand out.

We get the ordering out of the way fairly quickly. The one tip I was given about these lunches from the agent I apprenticed with was that you should match courses with the other diner. What this means is that if the editor orders an appetizer, I should order something light, even if it's a salad. The same goes for dessert, but I'll offer to share or split something if I'm comfortable with the editor. And I don't order an alcoholic beverage unless they do. The flip side of this is that if the editor orders a drink, I should have one. I once had lunch with a foreign agent who polished off a whole bottle of wine over lunch, while I nursed a single glass. It was known in the business that he never worked after lunch, and I was later told a story about how he had held an auction one afternoon after lunch and couldn't remember the deal points the next morning.

The agent I apprenticed under tells an indignant story about going to lunch with an editor who was on a liquid diet. The editor refused to eat a thing, which made the agent feel like a glutton for eating in front of her. Needless to say, that was not a very productive lunch.

The days of three-martini lunches, or even steak-and-potato lunches, are long gone. Alcohol and heavy food are hard work for a busy afternoon. We all tend to eat fairly light these days, which is why Japanese restaurants are a favorite.

Ordering

The chitchat around placing the order is often about the books the editor has brought, a deal one of us is currently negotiating, or even why we chose the entree or appetizer we did ("I just got back from Barcelona" or "I'm editing a goat cheese cookbook"). We both know that the purpose of this light conversation is to establish who we are and what our interests are without going directly into the hard sell on either end.

The kind of information I learn about an editor during this time can be anything from how many young children they have at home, where they've traveled recently or what their favorite TV program is to what they think about current events. During this time I find out who's into gardening or who owns a horse, all of which I file away in my memory, knowing that one day this information will prove to be very useful.

The Appetizers

When the appetizers arrive, we usually begin the second stage of getting to know each other, which covers how we got into publishing. This is very important information. I learn where an editor came from geographically (so I know who to send novels about the South to), what their educational background is, what their interests were before publishing (acting, NASA, film critic) and how they got their present job. How I use this information is all part of the matchmaking process. For instance, I once had a book about Hispanics at Harvard, and one group of editors I decided to send it to were Ivy League graduates. My lunches were invaluable there.

The Main Course

At about the time the main course arrives, the conversation should be shifting to the kind of books the editor is interested in buying. While this should be a fairly straightforward answer, it's often more complicated because an editor will tell you the kind of books she'd *like* to buy, which may be different than the kind of book she's been *told* to buy. I have to make sure that I ask both of these questions.

While most editors understand what I'm asking them, some editors answer with platitudes such as "best-sellers." One editor actually answered this question with the response "First novels that can sell 100,000 copies," to which I replied, "Oh, I have a whole pile of them in my office, and I had no idea where to send them." Thankfully, he got my sarcasm.

Today's editors have been told to look for products, not authors or books. They often tell me that they're looking for an author with a "platform," which means someone who already has a series of seminars, pamphlets, audiotapes and other tie-ins that the publisher is hoping can be used as a springboard to build their book sales on.

This point in the lunch is also where I tell editors about the books that I'm currently offering or that I will be sending out shortly. I try to match this list to common interests we've found during the lunch. I usually seriously pitch a few books at this time, and the editor lets me know if she wants me to send anything. Occasionally she'll be so enthused that she'll tell me she's sending a messenger, which means I have to rush back to the office to package the book up.

Coffee Time

We always order coffee or tea, but rarely have any dessert. Coffee time is where we wrap up our business. My business partner and I save our two biggest business questions for this time, when the editor's attention is no longer focused on the food on her plate.

This is where we explain to editors that for the past three years a large part of our business has been in developing books for editors on request. We tell the editor to take the client list back to her office to see if there are any authors she'd like to work with. Often, ideas for books are brought up at editorial meetings, and we can have our authors work up book proposals from these ideas. About a third of our business is done this way now, and we have managed to develop both fiction and nonfiction books this way.

We follow up that train of thought with what we like to think is our $64,000 question: "If the book fairy could grant you three wishes, what would they be?" Most editors are intrigued by this question, and even if they can't answer it on the spot (you'd be surprised at the number of editors who have been dreaming about certain kinds of books), they often call a few days after the lunch with additional book ideas.

If I know the editor or we've done a lot of business before, the lunch will have a much more personal feel. I've actually been doing business with some of these people for fifteen years, so I can ask them how their children are and how the renovation on the summer home is going, but I essentially cover the same bases every time I go to lunch:

What are you looking for?
What have you been told to buy?
What have you bought recently?
What do you really want to buy?

Although there's a wonderful free flow to these lunches, they tend to last two hours—too much less is rude, and too much longer keeps both of us from returning to our work. Recently, *The New York Times* reported that some bigshot editors were trying to double up on lunches by having two meals back to back in the two-hour slot, scheduling one agent for the appetizer and another for the main course (or another appetizer). I doubt that this is a large trend, because I'm not sure that many of us have the stamina for ten lunches a week.

The Check
Unless the agent is a real buffoon or the publishing house is extremely small, the editor will pick up the lunch tab for the agent. (The editor will be reimbursed for the cost of the lunch by his publisher and is usually given a corporate credit card to charge the lunches. The cost of the lunch is a tax deductible write-off for the publisher.) There are exceptions, however: One male agent hit on the female editor at lunch—and she stuck him with the tab. Prior to becoming an agent, my business partner worked for such a small publishing company that he had to justify every lunch he took and was given a hard time if he had more than four a month or if the tab went over $40 for two people in New York City.

Lunch Isn't Easy
My agency recently took on a new agent who came from the marketing side of cable television. At first she was thrilled to

go to lunch with editors at all these different midtown restaurants, but six months into the job, she commented that the lunches were the hardest part of the job, but also the most important. Looking at the sales she's made, she found that she had a much better idea of which editors were likely to click with a book or author as a result of having met them. Without the lunches, she was flying blind.

This chapter is very New York-centric, and obviously there are many successful literary agents who operate outside of the city. However, most of them have put in years in the tristate area and still come in monthly for a whirlwind of lunches and meetings. I know of one agent based in Minneapolis who flies into New York monthly and has twenty meetings over a three-day period.

YOUR EDITORIAL LUNCHES

When a writer meets with his editor, it too is serious business. While the lunch will not follow a pattern as formal as that between an agent and an editor (which is quite comfortable and casual, despite appearances), there are basic rules of business lunch etiquette that should be followed, as well as individual business issues that should be addressed.

As with the agent/editor lunch, the editor usually picks the restaurant and time and pays the tab. Even though it's expected, always thank your editor for taking you to lunch.

Although you don't have to match each other course for course, you should be aware of what your editor is eating versus what you are ordering, and remember that she has to go back to work, so she probably doesn't want to share a bottle of wine or a heavy dessert. The lunch should not run longer than two hours, unless your editor tells you that she has cleared the afternoon for you.

Editors meet with authors at different times during the writing of a book, so the editorial lunch can have differing purposes. If you've just sold the book, the lunch should focus on the writing and where you and your editor want the book to go. You might mention what you want to do in the future, but do not focus the lunch on the next book.

If the lunch has been scheduled because you or your editor are having concerns over the structure of the book, then the editorial content of the book is the focus of the lunch. The lunch is a good opportunity for you to try out alternative ways to solve an editorial problem without having to write them up first. This might also be when you would discuss how the book has changed since the contract was signed.

If you've delivered your book and are now meeting with your editor, you might use the lunch to talk about the rewrite or how to strengthen the book. For my first book I met with my editor, who had a long editorial letter waiting for me but delivered the points she needed to go over face to face, which softened the blow of hearing that I had a lot of work to do.

If you've delivered your manuscript and there is little to rewrite, then the lunch should definitely focus on the publisher's plans for your book and what you can do to help sell it. You should also bring up your ideas for future books and the direction you'd like to take your career. Make sure you go over all this with your agent first. If the two of you have developed a good relationship, your editor may even have a vested interest in working with you again and consequently may help you develop the next book into something that will fly at her editorial board. Lunch is a good place to launch trial balloons.

If you live near New York or travel to the city frequently, you might see your editor a couple of times during the year and a half it usually takes to go from signing the contract to publishing the book. However, many authors never meet with their editors.

THE AGENT/AUTHOR LUNCH

I like to meet with authors once I've sold their first book. I tend to think of this as a celebratory lunch. Occasionally I meet with authors when I've agreed to take them on, because I find it really does help everyone's confidence when you can put a face to a voice.

If I am just starting the process of submitting a book, the lunch will probably detail how I plan on selling the book and what the author can do to help me. As with meeting an editor, I'd like to learn a little bit about the author's other interests, just in case some interest or experience should come up that may become a book. However, I don't want to be overwhelmed with a resume of the author's last one hundred jobs.

If I'm meeting with an author to celebrate the sale of his book, my focus will be on the next stage of his career, in terms of both what he wants to write and how we can get the most mileage in house and in the bookstores.

The agent will usually choose the restaurant and time, because she knows where the good restaurants are near her office, and she should pick up the tab.

Just as in the editor/author relationship, how often you see each other depends on proximity and effort. If you live near New York, you will probably meet with your agent a number of times a year. If you live in an out-of-the-way area and don't travel much, you may only meet your agent once or twice in your writing career.

It is important to your career to meet with your agent, but you really only have to meet once. I have represented one author for more than twelve years and we've only met once. I have another client who lives within commuting distance to the city and takes classes here two days a week, and we see each other twice a month.

I really do try to meet all my clients, and if I haven't met someone after a few years, I might even agree to attend a writer's conference close to a writer's home just so I can meet with that client. For a meeting with a client whom I've only met once, I asked him to drive about two hundred miles when I was in Chicago, because I knew our chances of meeting again were slim unless we made the effort. His understanding of how important it was for us to meet and his willingness to seize the opportunity are two reasons why we've worked together so well for so long.

PART II
THE HUNT

CHAPTER SIX

How to Find the Right Agent

Researching the Field

Finding an agent can seem like an overwhelming task for a new writer.

It's much easier to find publishers. Just go to bookstores or libraries and examine book spines or your favorite author's title pages. However, just knowing the names of the publishers won't get you very far. Most major publishers no longer consider unsolicited manuscripts, so you have to find an agent who will take you on. It's a whole lot harder to find literary agents, who are not even listed separately in the New York business phone book.

When I go to writer's conferences, the panel discussions on agents are often filled to standing room only. Inevitably, a writer will raise his hand and ask just how an unpublished writer can expect to attract an agent. This question is often followed by the sad story of having sent the sole copy of the first one hundred pages of his novel to the most successful agent in publishing only to have it sent back within five days—unopened!

What's wrong with this picture? Everything.

Before you send out a single query letter, you need to do a lot of research. You need to know what agents are looking for, which agents are taking on new clients and the best way to approach them. All this information is readily available, but you must seek it out. If you don't do this legwork you are wasting your time, as well as that of the agents you approach.

If you are writing fiction, the absolute first thing you must do before you approach a literary agent is finish your novel. Nonfiction only requires a good query letter outlining your ideas and credentials. When I was a new agent (and therefore the person at the literary agency who read the slush), I would often ask to see the completed manuscript and have the author tell me that it would be finished in six months. I would always tell him to send it when it was completed, but by the time it arrived in my office, I had usually lost my enthusiasm for and interest in the novel. Sometimes the author never sent the manuscript because he never finished it. (How many unfinished novels are yellowing in desk drawers as I write this?) I quickly learned not to ask to read a first novel unless it was finished.

Next, buy or borrow from the library the annual *Writer's Market*, *Writer's Digest Guide to Literary Agents* or Jeff Herman's *Guide to Agents & Editors*. If you go the library route and these are reference titles, plan on spending at least an hour reviewing them. These guides to the book market tell you what is selling, what individual agents are looking for and how to approach them. Many of these books have articles written by agents describing what they do and what they want from writers. The books' editors also put together tips on how to attract these agents.

For instance, in my agency's entries in these books for 1999 you will learn that there are two agents in my agency (actually, we've just taken on a third agent—keep that in mind, and I'll tell you why in a moment). I specialize in dark fiction and pop culture in nonfiction, and my partner is looking for mysteries, thrillers and narrative nonfiction. We list examples of books we have sold in the past year. I mention that two things I am actively looking for are a "Latin Gone With the Wind" and ethnic urban horror. It also mentions that my agency is a member of the Association of Authors Representatives (AAR).

What does this mean to you, the writer? It should tell you just about everything you need to know about whether or not to send me a query letter.

If you've written a romance or a western, this listing should tell you that we are not the agency for you. It should also tell you that if you've written a witty analysis of the nuclear family in television it should go to me, but if you're working on the history of water it should be sent to my partner.

Sometimes these listings tell you who to send your work to. This is very important, because if a reference text tells you that there is someone at a literary agency actively taking on

---

☑ **PERKINS, RUBIE & ASSOCIATES, (IV)**, (formerly Perkins, Rabiner, Rubie & Associates), 240 W. 35th St., New York NY 10001. (212) 279-1776. Fax: (212) 279-0937. Contact: Lori Perkins, Peter Rubie, June Clark. Estab. 1997. Member of AAR, HWA. Represents 150 clients. 15% of clients are new/ previously unpublished writers. Perkins specializes in horror, dark thrillers, literary fiction, pop culture, Latino and gay issues (fiction and nonfiction). Rubie specializes in crime, science fiction, fantasy, off-beat mysteries, history, literary fiction, dark thrillers, narrative nonfiction. Clark represents humor, new age, women's issues and Jewish culture. Currently handles: 60% nonfiction books; 40% novels.

    ● Lori Perkins is the author of *The Cheapskate's Guide to Entertaining; How to Throw Fabulous Parties on a Budget* (Carol Publishing) and *How to Get and Keep the Right Agent for You* (Writer's Digest Books). Prior to becoming an agent, she taught journalism at NYU. Mr. Rubie is the author of *The Elements of Storytelling* (John Wiley) and *Story Sense* (Writer's Digest Books).

Represents: Nonfiction books, novels. Considers these nonfiction areas: art/ architecture/design; current affairs; commercial academic material; ethnic/cultural interests; music/dance/theater/film; science; "subjects that fall under pop culture—TV, music, art, books and authors, film, current affairs, etc." Considers these fiction areas: detective/police/crime; ethnic; fact-based historical fiction; fantasy; horror; literary; mainstream; mystery/suspense; psychic/supernatural; science fiction; dark thriller.

How to Contact: Query with SASE. Reports in 3-6 weeks on queries with SASE; 10 weeks on mss.

Needs: Obtains new clients through recommendations from others, solicitation, at conferences, etc.

Recent Sales: *Mojo Hurt*, by Greg Kihn (Forge); *Piercing the Darkness: Uncovering the Vampires in America Today*, by K. Ramsland (Harper); *The Science of Star Wars*, by Jeanne Cavelos (St. Martin's Press); *Keeper*, by Gregory Rucka (Bantam); *Witchunter*, by C. Lyons (Avon); *How the Tiger Lost Its Stripes*, by C. Meacham (Harcourt Brace).

Terms: Agent receives 15% commission on domestic sales; 20% on foreign sales. Offers written contract, only "if requested." Charges for photocopying.

Tips: "Sometimes I come up with book ideas and find authors (*Coupon Queen*, for example). Be professional. Read *Publishers Weekly* and genre-related magazines. Join writers' organizations. Go to conferences. Know your market and learn your craft."

Our listing in the 2000 *Guide to Literary Agents* (Writer's Digest Books).

new clients, that's a golden opportunity. It means that they are building a client list, so they are more likely to take on new writers and help you polish work that may need rewriting.

When I began as an agent, I went through the slush of the agency where I worked and took on and sold fourteen first novels my first year. While I always take on new clients (at least five a year), and at least one of them is totally unpublished, I have never taken on as many new clients as when I was starting out. Therefore, if you learn through research, networking or even gossip that there is a new agent at an agency, this greatly increases your chances of getting a literary agent. New agents need to build a client list, and they have more patience for working with authors whose work needs crafting.

The listings in these writer's reference books also tell you how to submit your work. Most agents ask for a query letter with a self-addressed stamped envelope. Don't send more. Don't query by E-mail or fax, unless the agent specifically encourages you to do so in these listings.

Not all agents are listed in the books mentioned above, because there are agents who are no longer actively soliciting new clients. However, all agents can be found in *The Literary Marketplace*, which is the most comprehensive listing of literary agents (and people in publishing for that matter) in the United States. It is an annual trade paperback—published by the company that produces *Publisher's Weekly*—which lists every publisher, agent, periodical- and book-related venue in the U.S. It's the size of the Oxford English Dictionary and costs close to $200, so you'll probably want to review this at your local library.

Agent listings in the *LMP* (that's the publishing lingo for this tome) will tell you the name, address, agents' names (always check for spelling), memberships, foreign affiliates and whether agents charge reading fees and accept query letters. The listing is very basic, but the list is complete.

What do you do if you've written a romance or a western? There are certainly hundreds of agents who represent this kind of material. You can look through these listings for those who are looking for this kind of material, but the best way to find agents for a specific genre is to go to the genre writer's organization for those kind of books, such as Romance Writers of America (RWA) or Science Fiction Writers of America (SFWA). Most of these organizations have listings on the World Wide Web. Horror Writers of America even has a discussion on agents that you can read online.

If you know that you've written a genre novel, call the respective writer's organization and ask them to recommend an agent or to give you a list of agents who are looking for new writers in this genre. (Many writers have pretensions about their work and can't admit it's a genre novel—"It's a literary novel about a vampire." No, it's a horror novel.) You may have to join the organization to get this information, but if you are serious about getting published, membership in a professional writer's organization should be well worth the price. You can also join the chats on the Web sites of various writers' organizations, where you can read about the experiences of published members.

Writer's organizations also put you in touch with other writers who can help you get an agent. While most writers will not refer you to their agent (unless they've read your work), published authors in a field usually know new agents who are selling in their genre and may pass that information on to you. Also, established agents who are no longer looking for new clients may refer you to a newer colleague. These are invaluable leads.

Other ways to find an agent include doing a search on the World Wide Web, which will bring up a lot of interesting information on everything from writer's organizations to writer's chat rooms to book doctoring services to out and out con artists. (One writer's Web site was sued for misrepresentation because they took money and never attempted to market the writer's work—see "reading fees" later on in this chapter.) The Internet is an excellent resource, but remember that it is totally unregulated.

Another way to find an agent is to match up your book with

a published book. For instance, if your novel is a "humorous woman in jeopardy mystery" and you think the readers of Susan Isaacs' *Compromising Positions* might like your book, you might want to send a query to her agent. You would do this by finding out which publishing house published her novel and calling that company. Ask to speak to someone in editorial, and when you get someone on the switchboard, ask if they can tell you who the editor for Susan Isaacs is. You will then be connected with that editor's assistant, who should be willing to give you the name of Isaacs' agent.

Occasionally authors thank their agents in the acknowledgments of books, so if you have a favorite author and she's mentioned her agent, that's as good a recommendation as any I know.

Writer's organizations and writer's conferences are often a good way to network for information. If there's a conference or organization in your area, you might want to attend that conference or a meeting of that organization to see if you can get a few names or hear an agent speak.

Once you've reviewed a number of these publications (or done a search on the Web), you should have a list of ten to thirty agents who seem like promising candidates to represent you. While there is nothing wrong with sending all thirty agents a query letter, it's kind of expensive and you don't want to have to explain to a number of agents that you have already signed on with someone else because you took the first person who answered.

I would recommend that you go through your list and choose the top three candidates. Mail each of them a copy of your query, and then wait six to eight weeks. If you haven't heard back by then, send out a query to the next three candidates.

Make sure you include a line in your query letter that you have sent this query to a "few select agents." This lets prospective agents know that there are other agents looking at the material (this is what agents do when submitting multiple copies to editors). It's only common courtesy, and the agent will appreciate it later on (and you never want to burn a bridge before you've even walked across it). Some agents get bent out of shape about not knowing a writer has made a multiple submission, so this is an important detail. Sometimes things don't work out with the first or second agent, and you may choose to go back to someone who showed interest. They'll be more receptive if you've done things right.

Keeping in mind how busy agents are and how many query letters we receive, you can call, fax or write a second letter to an agency if you haven't heard anything in two months. You still might not get a response, because it is hard to match old mail to new mail or because your query was pulled from the slush to be reviewed by the head of the agency, who is too busy to take on new material at this moment.

Once you've heard from an agent and decided that you want to work with her, you have to send a follow-up letter, fax or phone call to all the agents you contacted and haven't yet heard from informing them that your work is no longer available. If an agent responds to a query, no matter how long after you sent it, you should send a note thanking her for her interest. You never know if you may want to approach her later in your career.

AVOIDING BAD AGENTS

At writer's conferences I am often asked how to tell a good agent from a bad agent. This is usually followed by the question: What do you think of reading fees?

If an agent is a member of a writer's organization or has a good reputation within an organization's membership, it's a good indication that he is a good agent.

Literary agents do not have to pass a test or take an oath of office. However, many of us have joined the Association of Author's Representatives (AAR), which requires that we sign a very basic canon of ethics. It requires that we make our living exclusively from selling books, that we charge no more than a 15 percent commission and that we pay our authors within thirty days of receipt of their monies. I would say that any agent who is a member of AAR is a reputable agent. Lack of membership in AAR does not mean that an agent is disreputable, however—some of us are just much more independent than others, and many don't live in the New York City area and therefore can't take advantage of the full benefits of the organization.

Reading fees are a dicey subject among agents, so much so that they were one of the reasons why the two professional organizations of literary agents were unable to unite for years. In 1996, the Society of Author's Representaives (SAR) and the International Literary Agents Association (ILLA) joined to become AAR. The AAR finally decided to create a grandfather clause to include those agents who already charged reading fees before all members were required to sign the new canon of ethics, but not allow any new members to charge reading fees. Their feeling on this was that agents should make their living from selling books, not reading them, editing them, packaging them or illustrating them, which are all different jobs than selling.

One AAR member who charges a reading fee defended this practice by reminding us that our time is worth money. I have solved that dilemma for myself by not reading material that fails to capture my imagination right away. This is what most agents do and is why agents often reject books based on the first page or even the query letter.

Many writers feel that agents don't give their work a chance because we make our decision on such a small amount of written material. If you feel your work picks up steam later on, you should rewrite the book. If you need editorial guidance to do so or you want a detailed review of your material, then you should consider paying a reader's fee. However, if you just want a simple yes or no from an agent because you feel your work is ready for submission, send it to the agents who don't charge a fee. If they see something redeeming in the book and it needs work, they will tell you so. You can then take a writer's workshop or hire a book doctor on your own.

The sleazy agent I once worked for charged reading fees.

At one time I was one of the readers, which was a good thing for the writers who paid me to read their work—I did go on to become a successful agent, so my three pages of advice to them were very professional. But there's no guarantee that the person who reads your book will be the agent herself, or even someone with a more professional background than your own. Often, readers are fellow unpublished writers.

I did take on one of the novels I was paid to read, and sold it. Another writer who paid us to read his manuscript later won a Whiting Award and was published by Farrar Straus & Giroux. But neither one of those authors needed to pay us first. They were both exceptional writers to begin with and could have easily gotten an agent without paying a fee.

Many writers think that if they pay the reader's fee they will have a better chance of being taken on by the agency. I like to think of that as The Publisher's Clearing House Approach to publishing (buy a magazine subscription and maybe Ed Mc-Mahon will ring your bell with a million-dollar check). That's not the way publishing should work. Your *writing* should open doors, not your money.

Another question that comes up at these writer's conferences: "Is it essential that an agent be in New York?" Remember, the book publishing industry is in New York, so a New York agent is more likely to have up-to-the-minute industry information.

That does not mean that good, successful literary agents don't exist outside of New York. Most regions have at least one good agent who works with local authors. (It's nice to be able to meet with your agent face to face, although most New York agents travel so often that we do manage to meet most of our clients.) Whether you choose a New York agent goes back to the decisions you have to make about whether you want to be a big fish in a little pond or a guppy in a great lake.

Once you know who the agents are, where to find them and what they say they want, it's time to craft the perfect query letter that will make them fall in love with your work before they've even read a single line of your book.

CHAPTER SEVEN

How to Interest an Agent

Killer Queries and Queries That Kill

Think of the process of finding an agent as like dating. You are embarking on a matchmaking experience that should pair you up with someone you may have a relationship with for years, if not for your entire writing career.

Finding an agent is therefore serious business. While we all dream of falling in love, most relationships last because the partners are truly well matched. Your relationship with your agent must be based on this same long-lasting glue.

So what you really want in an agent is someone who is not going to tell you that you are brilliant, but someone who truly understands your work and your vision for how you want to grow as a writer.

IMPRESSING AN AGENT

My suggestions for impressing the right agent are much the same as I would give to someone going out on a first date.

1. Put your best foot forward. You want to make an agent want to read more, and the way to do this is to keep your introduction short, with your most impressive information up front.

Agents are very busy and receive a ton of queries (my agency receives at least 1,000 a month). Your letter must be to the point and informative.

Never send a query letter that is longer than one page. Two hundred and fifty words should be more than enough for you to introduce yourself and your book. I have sold more than

2,000 books and have sent out as many pitch letters, and I have never sent a letter to an editor that was longer than one page. If I find myself writing a longer letter, I always edit.

2. Make a clean and professional first impression. A dirty, tattered, handwritten query letter is not going to get the same attention as a clean, well-presented letter. My partner won't even read a handwritten letter. It goes straight in the garbage.

Use white or cream-colored 8½″ × 11″ bond paper. If your paper is old and yellowed, buy new sheets. Don't use greeting cards or writing paper intended for personal letters. This is a professional relationship, not a quick letter to a friend. Never send a letter printed on erasable bond, because it smudges, often obliterating whole words and sentences.

Since I represent a lot of horror writers, I receive weird query letters. I've been sent letters on black stationery with white letters, queries handwritten in red ink that is supposed to look like blood, and all sorts of computer-generated home-made stationery with skulls, vampire bats and coffins as decorations. This is the sign of an amateur and does not impress me. (Actually, it makes me that much more skeptical of the writer's ability to take his work seriously.)

Never send a handwritten letter, no matter how clear you think your writing is. If you can, also type the envelope or label address. It just looks more professional. Type your letter following standard letter-writing format. Double-space everything you send. Use one-inch margins on all four borders of your letter.

Use 10- or 12-point type. Don't use script or fancy typefaces. Don't typeset your letter or sample chapters to make them look more like a book.

Don't send letters with mistakes. Make the change and print the letter again. A letter with a mistake hand-corrected by the author shows me that he didn't think I was important enough to take a minute to run the letter out again.

Also, always check the spelling of the agent's name and title. Some agents won't open letters that are misaddressed.

While I will take on someone who sends a query letter to Laurie Perkins, letters addressed to Mr. Perkins have an uphill climb.

3. Don't be cute or overly clever. Like the blood-dripping letters described previously, many authors try to get my attention with unusual queries. While I remember getting a query with a blood-dripping plastic axe, I don't remember the book—and I didn't take that author on.

Don't try to bribe the agent either. We've been sent wine, booze, Cuban cigars, coffee mugs and a box of Vidalia onions as enticements to represent writers, but none of those authors have made it that way. The work has to stand on its own.

Two memorably tasteless queries do stand out. A woman tried to "seduce" my business partner in her query letter, offering to "fondle his adjectives." She enclosed a black-and-white photograph of herself in a negligee.

Another author started his query with the line "I'm going to grab you and beat you senseless, Lori Perkins." He then went on to describe in detail the tortures his main character would inflict upon me, but I didn't read any further.

Obviously, we declined to represent both writers.

4. Don't tell him you love him on the first date. Some authors manage to get my attention in the first line or paragraph of their query letter, and then ruin that goodwill by saying they have ten completed novels in the closet that they want to send me. Or after I've asked to see sample chapters, they overnight me the material and then call every other day to see if I've read it. Or they tell me they plan on quitting their day job as soon as I take them on.

Sometimes, an author's enthusiasm and eagerness for success in his writing career can overwhelm an agent. Just as in a dating situation, it's best to be cautious until you know one another well.

5. Don't lie to impress. There's a famous story of an author who made up a quote from a best-selling writer, which his agent used to sell the book for a nice six-figure deal. When an article about the sale appeared, the published author called

The New York Times to announce that he had never read the book. The publisher rescinded his offer quite publicly.

It's just as impressive to say that you *might* be able to get a quote from Mary Higgins Clark as it is to have one, if you indeed know her (or her daughter, or a friend of a friend who has promised to approach her). Don't fudge the facts with your agent, especially on the first date.

6. At the beginning of the author/agent relationship, I don't want to hear about other agents you've sent the novel to. I don't need to know that you've tried to sell the book yourself and, now that it's been rejected by every editor listed in this year's *Writer's Market*, you thought you'd try getting an agent. This is another reason why the query letter should be short: It keeps the author out of trouble.

Don't spend your time talking about your ex-spouse. Authors have given me information way too early that I just don't need to know until we're well on the way to a solid author/agent relationship, much like a date who won't shut up about his first wife/ex-girlfriend.

I also don't want to hear about another writer's career (whether good or bad). Each writer's book is unique.

7. Know when it's time to go home. By this, I mean give the prospective agent enough time to read requested material without badgering her. If you must call to ask if she's read your material (after six to eight weeks, unless she's said she'll get to it sooner) and you do get her on the phone, don't keep her on it all day. Until an agent has agreed to take on your work, you don't need to know how she plans on marketing the book and who she's going to send it to.

Likewise, the agent doesn't need to know that you'll be running in the New York Marathon or going to your high school reunion this weekend—unless it relates to your book. Too much information early on is just useless and annoying.

8. Don't move too fast. Like the woman who imagines what her married name will be after the first date, don't start wondering how much you're going to get for the book or whether Steven Spielberg will be directing the movie himself, just because an agent has said they'll look at three chapters and an outline.

Don't get ahead of yourself. Don't make assumptions about the future until you know there will *be* a future.

9. Don't forget to give her your number. You would be surprised at the number of authors who don't include their telephone numbers in their query letters. Always include your phone number, address and E-mail address, if you have one.

And, of course, always enclose a self-addressed, stamped envelope or postcard if you really want a response. Many agents just throw away a query letter (and the accompanying manuscript) if it doesn't have an SASE.

Just recently I was sent a certified letter from a woman who works with the FBI on high-profile cases. She obviously thought I was important enough to go to the trouble of making sure the Post Office notified her when I received the letter (this is not necessarily a great idea—it just means that someone at the agency signed for the material, not necessarily the agent herself), but she failed to give me a phone number to reach her. Her personal phone number was unlisted, so the only way I had of getting in touch with her was to send her a letter via her SASE. She was lucky that I was that interested in her work. I'm sure other agents just threw the whole thing away.

10. Be punctual. Just like going on a date, if you say you're going to be somewhere, be there on time. Call if you're going to be late.

What this means in your relationship with an agent is that if you say you're going to send something that the agent has requested, you should send it right away. If there's some kind of delay, let the agent know.

KILLER QUERIES

OK, so now that you know who to approach, how to present your material and what to avoid, how do you get an agent to want to see some of your work? By writing a killer query letter.

The best query letters are short and informative and show that the writer has done some research and knows his field.

Let's take a look at two killer query letters, and then I'll tell you why they work.

For a Novel

My idea of the perfect query letter for a novel would be the following:

> Dear Lori Perkins:
>
> Through my membership in Horror Writers of America, I know that you are looking for an urban ethnic horror novel, which is exactly what *The Harlem Horror* is.
>
> Set in Manhattan's most famous neighborhood, *The Harlem Horror* is a ghost story about four generations and the secret they have kept in their Harlem brownstone.
>
> I'm an active member of HWA, where I've met some of your clients, including Chris Golden, who has said he would read my manuscript. I've published four short stories in various horror magazines and anthologies.
>
> Please let me know if you would like to see the first three chapters and the outline of my completed manuscript.

This straightforward letter of about 150 words covers all the bases. It tells me that the author is serious about his writing (he's a member of Horror Writers of America and active in the organization), that he's done enough research to know the kinds of books I represent, who I represent and what I'm looking for, and that he's been writing long enough to have published four short stories.

This author briefly describes what his novel is about in one sentence, which is actually perfect. Most agents don't need a long, detailed synopsis. When we pitch a novel to editors, when they pitch it at their editorial meetings, and then when the book is pitched to the bookstores and foreign publishers, the more succinct the plot, the better.

My business partner, Peter Rubie, always says that the best novel synopsis is one sentence long, because it shows that both the author and the book are focused. He calls this the *What if?* exercise, wherein the author tells the story beginning with those two words. I've found that the word *suppose* also works as the starting point for this exercise.

For example, this is his synopsis of the best-selling novel *Shogun* by James Clavell. "What if an English sailor is shipwrecked off the coast of Japan and becomes a pawn in a power play to take over the island?"

Rubie also says that if an author is unable to describe his novel in one sentence, then perhaps the book still needs work.

For Nonfiction

For nonfiction, I usually need a little more background on the author, because I often have to pitch his credentials as well as his writing experience. Since nonfiction is sold on the basis of a proposal (whereas first novels are almost all sold based on the completed manuscript), the more of a publishing track record the author has, the better.

Below is the epitome of a nonfiction query letter for me. It is so perfect that, even though I received it at a time when it was impossible for me to take on new clients, I called the author and asked him to wait three months until I could take it on—and then I sold it in three weeks.

> Dear Lori Perkins:
>
> I want you to be my agent. I know the kind of books you do and I think you would be the perfect agent for *Godzilla's Unauthorized Biography*.
>
> *Godzilla's Unauthorized Biography* would be the first western book published on this nuclear-age monster. With the big-budget Godzilla movie coming out next year, the timing for an American book on Godzilla is just right.
>
> I am a reporter for *The Los Angeles Times*, and

I've written extensively on pop culture for a number of newspapers and magazines.

I have been an avid Godzilla fan since I was a child, and have visited Japan to do research for this book.

Again, this query letter told me everything I needed to know about this project—what it was about, who the author was and what his credentials for writing this book were, and that he had researched the field and knew who I was and what I did. Since he had enclosed the proposal, I called him to let him know that I was interested in representing him. We had to edit the proposal because he told me that there might be problems with photo rights (I had him include that information in the proposal so that the publisher would know that we needed a large photo budget on this book, which we got), and we also added more information on the upcoming movie.

Your chances of getting picked up by an agent are better if you have published something (even an article or short story) in your field, because it shows that someone else thought your work was worthy of publication. So you might try selling something to the local newspaper or a small press before you begin looking for an agent for your book.

However, you should never feel that your work will not be considered just because you have never been published. There are other considerations, such as working or studying in the field (you're writing a novel about dinosaurs and you're a paleontologist at the Museum of Natural History) or even a lifelong interest in the subject.

Although most writers tell me more than I want to know (I really don't need to know what your high school English teacher thought about the novel unless she is a best-selling author), some authors are reticent about their accomplishments. I represent one literary writer who waited until the day before I sent out her work to mention to me that she had studied with Tobias Wolfe and that she had received a fellowship in creative writing from Columbia University.

KNOW YOUR STRENGTHS

Sometimes an accomplished professional sends me a query for a novel based on the field that they work in, and it is obvious that they should be writing nonfiction. It takes time to learn how to craft a good novel; it is easier to write nonfiction, and often easier to get published in nonfiction.

One of my authors who had a doctorate in philosophy, taught existentialism and science fiction on a university level and had a master's in clinical psychology came to me to represent her novel. After reading the book, which needed work, and meeting her, it became obvious to me that she should be writing nonfiction. During the course of our conversation she mentioned that she was fascinated by the existential elements in Anne Rice's vampire novels and wondered if Rice had included them on purpose. I told her to call Rice, who was listed in the phone book at the time. After a two-hour conversation with Rice, she called to ask if I thought there was a market for Anne Rice's authorized biography. We sold it soon afterward. The author has since gone on to write eight more books and is still working on her novel, which is eagerly awaited by her reading public now that she has a following.

Another of my authors was an editor at a publishing house who had the same taste as me when it comes to fiction. Over the course of three years, I must have sold her thirty novels. So I was quite upset when she informed me that she was leaving publishing, but pleased when she asked me to represent her. Of course she wanted to write fiction (she had a very good science fiction novel), but what she forgot to mention was that before she became a book editor she had been an astrophysicist at NASA (she wrote the manual for the space shuttle), so it was easier for me to sell very commercial popular science books by her. We have sold some fiction, too, but she makes much more money with the nonfiction.

My business partner calls fiction the "siren on the rocks" for nonfiction writers, and I agree with him. I can't tell you the number of commercial nonfiction books I've sold by people who came to me with their novels and didn't realize that their knowledge and experience were more unique (and profitable) in nonfiction.

CHAPTER EIGHT

SELLING YOURSELF

*How to Write a Nonfiction Proposal
or a Novel Synopsis*

You may be able to sell a novel without writing a synopsis, but it is just about impossible to sell a nonfiction book without a proposal. Even Bill Gates had to put something down on paper to get his seven-figure advance.

Both synopses and proposals are sales tools. It is the writer's ad for his book and, like an ad, it needs to be clever and memorable and make someone want to buy the product.

Proposal and synopsis writing is therefore an essential skill for anyone who intends to get published. Most of the time, the difference between a $5,000 and a six-figure book deal is in the proposal or synopsis itself. If well crafted, it will get you a larger advance and more serious treatment from your editor and the various people you will have to deal with in marketing and publicity. It can even get you a better book jacket, because the designer can understand what the book is about.

THE NONFICTION PROPOSAL

Proposal writing is a lot of work; many of my authors have rewritten their proposals three times before we even begin the submission process. The great thing about writing a proposal, however, is that you don't have to write the entire book first. Most nonfiction is sold on proposal, which means that you know how much you will be paid for the book before you even write it, and your publisher will give you some money (usually half the advance) to live on while you write the book. That should certainly provide inspiration.

Your proposal is your resume and the blueprint for your book all rolled into one, so you need it to be as complete, professional and entertaining as you can make it (even if it's about the history of embalming in America). Your proposal must intrigue your editor and inspire her to take it before the editorial board, where it will be dissected and analyzed by others who do not see it as a work of art or a conduit of essential information but as a commodity. You need to have all the potential sales information readily available so your editor can quickly answer the marketing department's eternal questions of who will buy this book and why, as well as how many units they can sell and whether the author can get on *Oprah*.

My business partner likes to think of literary agenting as the selling of ideas, but the bottom line is that you can't copyright an idea. It's all in the presentation. Ten writers could take the same idea for a book, and each book would be totally unique. That's why it is unrealistic to fear that an editor will steal your idea and give it to another writer (or take it for herself). No two books on the same subject could ever be identical (or there would certainly be no market for this book, because dozens of books on getting published are printed every year).

Your book proposal must reflect your voice and style so that your editor will know how the book will read. Be yourself in your proposal or your editor will be expecting something else when the finished book arrives.

Although you can't sell a book on the idea alone, you can get an agent interested in representing you based on your idea for a book if you are focused on what you want to write. If you are an expert in your field or a celebrity of some sort, an agent might even be willing to come up with a book idea for you and help craft the proposal or put you together with a ghost writer, but that's the exception to the rule. There are even professional proposal writers whom you can pay to develop your idea for you.

Nonfiction book proposals follow a format that I will give to you in a moment. However, I can't emphasize enough that the author's style and personality must come through in the proposal. A dry proposal on cornering the stock market just won't sell as well (meaning as quickly or for as much) as a hip guide to Wall Street for the new millennium.

In addition to a strong personal writing style, your proposal must have good, solid organization. There must be an obvious beginning, middle and end to your proposed book and a structure on which your material is supported. There must be a real progression of information and a premise that you explore during the course of the book.

When I am writing a book proposal, the first thing I work on is the chapter-by-chapter outline of the book. I know my book idea is strong enough to support 60,000 to 80,000 words (which is the length of the average book published today) if I can successfully come up with twelve to twenty-five chapters on the subject. I often rearrange those chapters as the outline for the book comes together, but I find I have a much firmer idea of just exactly what will be in my book and how long the book will be if I basically outline first.

There is no rigid number of pages for a book proposal. I have sold books on two-page outlines and sixty-page proposals. However, on average, book proposals run between ten and twenty pages, with additional pages for sample chapters or a writing sample.

The size of your book proposal depends on the subject matter of the book, as well as who the author is. The proposal for a 50,000 word biography of nineteen-year-old actress Jennifer Love-Hewitt was only a few pages long—an outline of her life, how the author was going to obtain Love-Hewitt's baby pictures and when the author could deliver. The fact that the author was a well-respected writer of pop biographies was enough of an author bio.

The proposal for a book on the reality of the computers used in the *Star Trek* universe, on the other hand, ran more than thirty pages, with a lot of emphasis placed on who the author was (a revered computer programmer and hacker who has published science fiction). The author's contacts in the computer and science fiction fields were essential to selling and marketing this book, so much more attention (and consequently more pages) was given to those areas of this proposal.

Writing the Nonfiction Book Proposal

Nearly every nonfiction book proposal includes the following elements, although sometimes two categories are combined.

1. Title Page
2. Overview
3. Market Analysis and Comparable Books
4. Table of Contents
5. Expanded Table of Contents
6. About the Author
7. Sample Writing
8. Additional Media Information (articles, video clips, portfolio, etc.)

Any author who knows my tastes and interests and follows this format is bound to have his proposal reviewed seriously by me. I would say the same goes for any other agent in the business.

Title Page. This should be self-explanatory, but let me go over the basics. Your proposal must have a title. It doesn't have to be the title that ends up on the book (and it probably won't be), but it has to be something better than "Untitled Book About Lawyers." If you don't even bother to come up with a working title, it shows a certain laziness on your part—and who wants to work with a lazy author?

Your title should be no longer than ten words. Use a subtitle (which should be no longer than fifteen words) if you feel you have to dress up or explain the title. However, if your subtitle is convoluted or too clever, this could be a warning sign that your title doesn't work.

Center the title in the middle of a blank page. Center the subtitle under it. Center your name under that.

If you have an agent, put your agent's name, company name, address, phone number and fax number in the lower right-hand corner of your title page. If you don't have an agent, put your name, address, day and evening phone numbers, fax number and E-mail address in the lower right-hand corner.

Overview. This is one of the most important sections of your proposal, so don't rush it—and don't try to fake it.

Your book overview should hook the editor in the first paragraph, and then expand upon that hook. Many proposals start with a fascinating quote, an incredible statistic, an anecdote or even a question, all of which should relate directly to the book.

Once you have hooked the reader, you have to lay out your cards. This is no time to be coy or misleading. Tell your editor exactly what you expect to do in this book and how you plan on doing it (for example, the research you will do and how the information will be gathered).

Your proposal should include the book's features (I will interview fifty rookie baseball players throughout the country over six months through my fellowship at Columbia University) as well as the book's anticipated results (to examine how the American baseball dream has changed as we approach the twenty-first century). Book proposal overviews should run between two and six pages. Anything longer than that can, and should, be edited back.

When I was a rookie agent, I knew a freelance reporter who had been covering a story for nine years. He was considered the national expert, and every newspaper that ran a story on the subject ended up consulting him, and usually asking him to write an article for them. I quickly realized that this journalist probably had a book in him and called with an invitation for representation. Alas, he already had an offer for a book from an academic publisher for a very low advance based on a sixty-page, single-spaced proposal. He was unhappy with the offer, so I suggested he let me look over the proposal to see if I thought a trade publisher might be interested.

The proposal was turgid. I don't think I even finished reading it, and this story had layers of scandal and political espionage. So I had him rewrite the proposal. We carved it down to twelve double-spaced pages, and the book sold in auction within two weeks for fifteen times what the academic publisher had offered.

The last paragraph of your overview should include an estimate of how many pages the manuscript will be and when you believe you can deliver it.

If the book lends itself to an unusual format, or if there are a lot of illustrations or permissions, you must include this information here. For instance, a proposal for an illustrated book often gives the approximate number of photographs, how many will be black and white or color and even the suggested trim size.

Market Analysis and Comparable Books. Most of the proposals that come to me over the transom need the most work in this area. Authors seem to be afraid to research their field. Many authors tell me they don't know how to do this (and many of my writers are journalists for the nation's leading newspapers), but there's no excuse for a weak marketing section if you have Internet access.

The marketing analysis is a very important part of the book proposal. It is where your editor will be looking for responses to give to the marketing department, and without good statistics and information at her fingertips, the sale will be lost.

The marketing information your editor expects to find here includes figures on who will read (and buy) this book. No one can really answer that question truthfully, but you can extrapolate by getting membership numbers for professional organizations, sales on previous books or media-related items that compare with your book, box office figures for movies even tangentially related to your topic, fan club memberships, census figures and recent poll results—you name it. You're a writer: Be creative! A little ingenuity in this area could be the difference between your unpublished book and a contract.

But don't lie, and don't make up the figures. Don't fudge either—your editor (or the marketing department) can look something up on the Internet just as quickly as you can.

A good marketing section includes an honest evaluation of comparable books on the market. This usually includes anywhere from three to ten books, usually published within the last five years, but sometimes you can cite the best-sellers of the 1970s to make the point, for example, that there hasn't been a big haunted house book since *The Amityville Horror*.

You should list each book's complete title, author, publisher, year of publication, type of publication (hardcover, trade or mass market paperback) and a brief description of the book. You should also include a line about how your book is different from these others.

During the course of researching your book market, you might find there is a book that sounds exactly like yours. Don't panic. As I said before, no two writers can cover the subject in the same way. So order the book from the library or a bookstore, read it, and then include a brief explanation of why your book is better than the one that's already out there. You might have to shift your book's focus a little to make sure that your niche is indeed unique.

The best way to research comparable books is through *Books in Print*, which is an annual listing of all the books that are still available for purchase. Some of my authors have been using Amazon.com and Barnesandnoble.com in the same way, but they're not as comprehensive and do not list all the information you should include in this section. However, they will give you a book's ranking, which you can't get from *Books in Print*.

Remember, just because a book is in print doesn't mean that it is easy to buy. Therefore, if all your competition is published by small presses, you might want to mention that the subject has been published by the small press, and that means that the time is right for a more commercial book on the topic.

If a lot of books have been published on your topic, you can just say something like "many titles on angels have been published in the past few years, including (cite some well-known titles here), but my book will be unique in that it is the first to . . ." and then detail why your book is different and/or why you are the only one who can write this book. Be as specific as possible.

Never pretend that there are no previously published books on your topic. A book that has no competitors or predecessors probably doesn't have an audience.

Some authors are under the impression that the marketing section of a proposal is where they make suggestions for how the publisher should market their book. Wrong. Unless the author is a marketing professional and has extensive media contacts, this is the sign of an unprofessional author. The thrashing out of the actual marketing plan for the book is best done when the book is finished. Otherwise, it is the tail wagging the dog.

If, however, the author is an exceptional speaker or national lecturer with tons of local and national media contacts, you might want to break this section of the book proposal into two parts, with the marketing section emphasizing just how the author can target his audience. Possible quotes, introductions or forwards from famous people, national endorsements, special sales possibilities, the author's national tour schedule and so on should all be included in this section.

Also included in this section would be any seasonal or tie-in considerations, such as those for a Christmas or Halloween book, or when the big-budget Godzilla movie is expected to be released so that the author's book can be on the bookshelves when audiences leave the theaters.

Table of Contents. This is the heart of your book. A poorly constructed table of contents will make an editor reject the book even if she loves the topic.

As mentioned previously, the average nonfiction book will have twelve to twenty-five chapters. Of course, some books have fifty short chapters, but again, that's unusual. For your first published book, try to stick to the norm unless you have a good reason for deviating from it.

Each chapter should have a title of its own, which should be descriptive, self-explanatory and clever all at the same time.

You should include a one- or two-sentence description of what will be in each chapter. For a more serious book, if you have already done some of the research or have some of the findings, you might want to include this where it is appropriate. However, your chapter descriptions should never run more than a page each.

Sample Chapter or Writing Sample. This is not as simple as it sounds. There are quite a lot of choices to be made, and it is important for the author to make the best choices for him and for his book here.

For a nonfiction book, it really doesn't matter which chapter the author includes. Often the first chapter is the least exciting, because it is an overview of the book, which the author has more or less already included in the beginning of the proposal. One thing you definitely want to avoid in your proposal is redundancy.

When my authors ask me which chapter they should include, I suggest that they write the chapter they can finish (never leave notes in your proposal stating that you will fill in this information when you have done the research). However, it is also important that the author write the chapter that would be of greatest interest to the editor.

For instance, I represent a writer who is working on a book on the cultural history of masturbation. She has completed the research for the chapter on the invention and development of the vibrator (she even visited a vibrator museum in San Francisco), but the chapter that would be most interesting to her editor (and the marketing department) is the one on how masturbation has been portrayed in popular culture through books, TV and film.

Sheree Bykofsky, an agent colleague of mine who has also written a book on getting published, suggests that the author always include an upbeat chapter. This is great advice—as long as it is also the chapter that will interest the editor most.

Occasionally there is a shortcut to writing a whole chapter. If you have a portion of a chapter that is complete on its own, you may only have to submit that. If you've published an article on the subject of your book recently (within the past five years), you can also submit that as your writing sample. That's what I did to sell this book. I included the article I wrote on agenting for the *1994 Writer's Digest Guide to Literary Agents*. However, sometimes an editor will still ask for some writing from the actual book, so you should know which chapter you will work on should this request be made.

About the Author. This section is also one where the author might find himself facing more choices than he expected. In general, the author bio should run about a page. It should include the most relevant material to the book topic first, such as the author's professional or educational accomplishments that enable him to write the book. The next line or paragraph should detail the author's writing history or educational credits. Awards, quotes and earlier career accomplishments should follow. A line at the end of the bio might include family history, the author's hometown, or some whimsical hobby or interest, if it's appropriate.

However, if the author is an extremely media-savvy promotional speaker or seminar promoter, this is the place to include all that relevant information, such as how many seminars the author does a year, where his biggest markets are, some of his biggest clients, quotes from some of his most successful lectures by CEOs and the like.

I have found that some of my authors are surprisingly modest when it comes to their bios. This is not the time for humility. Unless you have a list of achievements and awards a mile long, include every one from the poetry contest you won in high school to your second-place award in the local cheesecake bakeoff (especially if you are writing a cookbook).

Sometimes first-time authors don't think they have much of a background to write about, and consequently emphasize only their professional achievements. They forget to tell me that they've been featured in their college alumni newsletter or that they took creative writing classes with some best-selling author in the 1980s. You should always include writing-related experience, even if it is only that you've been an active member of a local writer's workshop for the past three years.

Additional information. There is a finite amount of additional material you can add to a proposal, but it's different for each book. This would include articles you've written about the subject, articles about you or articles about the subject from major publications (*Time* or *The New York Times*) to show the popularity or timeliness of your topic. Your most recent book might also be included to show that you can finish a book. This would also include any video clips of TV appearances you've made recently, as well as brochures about you or your service, ads featuring you or your service, self-published books and audiocassettes. If the author is very attractive, and this has something to do with the proposal (a former model writing about the inside dirt on the fashion industry), you might include author photos.

If the book is heavily illustrated or is a photo or art book, you would put together a portfolio with sample photographs or three two-page spreads of illustrations and text.

As I mentioned previously, sometimes it takes two or three tries to get the proposal right. Often, one or two editors will make very good suggestions on a book proposal, and I will pull the submission and have the author retool the proposal. I will then send it exclusively to the editor(s) who made the suggestions.

For this book, I originally wanted to write a book about etiquette for writers, but I was told that the niche was too small. My editor said he wanted a book on agenting, though, which I quickly put together. However, my proposal was geared to the published author, and Writer's Digest Books are bought by a lot of new writers. So I rewrote the proposal again with a slant toward the beginning writer. The third time was the charm.

WRITING THE FICTION SYNOPSIS

For the unpublished novelist, there is no shortcut to a book sale without writing the complete manuscript first. However, once you have sold your first novel, you should be able to sell your next books based on a detailed outline and three sample chapters, so the time put into learning how to write a killer synopsis is never wasted.

The first person who is likely to ask to see your novel synopsis is a prospective agent. What an agent is looking for is a well-paced, plot-driven outline that clearly tells the beginning, middle and end of the novel. All the plot twists must be explained. This should be no longer than ten pages and could be as short as two, if you can do it succinctly.

For some reason, some writers have been led to believe it's wise to leave the editor or agent guessing as to who did it or what the motivation of the characters was. Your plot synopsis is an outline, not jacket copy or a review. You must tell all.

Start your synopsis with a brief overview of the story, followed by a detailed outline. It's better to write a dry chapter-by-chapter outline than to meander all over the place, picking up and discarding plot twists and characters without explaining how they fit in. Remember, you will be sending sample chapters as well, so your writing itself will speak for your literary ability: The outline is only there to tell the agent or editor where you plan on going with your book and how you plan on getting there.

However, if you're confident about your writing, you could add examples of fiction techniques to the synopsis, such as a bit of dialogue or some interior monologue. This can help spice up a dry outline.

Some writers include a page on the major characters in their novels. I believe this is a device they've borrowed from the theater and Hollywood, but it does absolutely nothing for me. I usually don't read it and consider it a waste of paper.

As I've explained, when a writer is asked to send three chapters (or fifty pages), it is understood that he will be sending the *first* three chapters. There is no option of which pages to send for fiction.

If a writer is well published in any venue or has studied seriously, he might want to include a writer's bio with his synopsis and sample chapters. A list of writers he can approach for possible quotes could be included here as well (these should be people you have some possibility of getting in touch with, not a wish list). If the author is a former rock star (hey, it could happen—I represent 1980s gold-record winner Greg Kihn) or a personal trainer writing a murder mystery series, he might want to include a photograph.

Sometimes an agent sends out a partial manuscript with a synopsis when the author is interested in changing publishers (or when the publisher has failed to pick up the author's option). This might also be the case if the novel is extremely high concept and the author is well connected to the subject, such as a what-if novel about The Beatles written by their former manager, Alan Klein.

The optimal situation for the agent would be for the writer to give her one hundred pages (about a third of the book), which should be enough to ensure that the editor's colleagues won't send the partial manuscript back to the agent with a request to see it again when it's complete (this is happening more and more). The writer would then have the option of writing a synopsis that picks up where the partial manuscript left off or writing an encapsulation of the entire plot. My personal preference is for the first option.

I have included both a sample nonfiction proposal and a novel synopsis in the appendix of this book. However, if you would like to examine other proposals and/or novel synopses, you should approach the membership of a writer's organization. The group itself might have some samples, or you could ask members if they would share theirs with you. If you're in a writer's workshop or you network with other writers, this is also something they should be able to show you.

Don't be shy. All writers need a helping hand at some point in their career. Just remember that what comes around, goes around. Once you've taken a sip from the well of a writer's guidance, you owe the writing universe your time and patience when you're approached by a younger, newer writer for advice. And if you're lucky, it will happen to you sooner than you thought.

CHAPTER NINE

WHAT TO EXPECT FROM YOUR AGENT

The Basics, as Well as Setting Goals and Priorities

The waiting is over: You have an agent. Someone has agreed to take you on as a client and send out your work. Now what?

The first thing your agent might do is ask you to revise your manuscript or proposal. This may seem unbelievably frustrating, because it took so long to get an agent, but your agent knows what she's talking about. The average agent with ten years of experience has sold more than a thousand books, so you can trust her judgment when she says a 600-page murder mystery is a hard sell or you have to do more market research for your proposal. Even seasoned professional writers have to revise their work before it goes out. That's one of the things you pay an agent for.

Once your agent is ready to begin submitting your work, you should discuss the terms of her representation. (What's her commission? Does she charge for expenses?) If you have any questions about how she sells things and what her expectations are for the book, this is the time to ask. Neither one of you wants surprises halfway through the contract process.

This is one of the reasons many agents have agency agreements that they ask all their clients to sign. The agreement lays out the terms of their representation and puts on paper what the agent expects from the writer. However, it usually doesn't cover the writer's concerns, so do not look there for a blueprint of how your agent will submit your work.

Agency agreements are a standard practice in our business,

although they are not uniform. Of the three agencies I've worked in, two used agency agreements. I do not.

Agency agreements, when they are used, are fairly straight-forward and should run between two and five pages. Anything longer than that should set off alarms. (Look out for a clause in there about your firstborn.)

Agency agreements usually cover one book or a period of time, such as one year from the date of signing. The agreement should lay out the terms of your agent's representation with regard to domestic commission (U.S. and Canada), which is 10 or 15 percent; foreign commission, which is 20 to 30 percent because we split the commission with other agents in foreign countries; and film commissions, which are 10 to 15 percent. The agreement should also lay out exactly what expenses (if any) your agent expects you to compensate her for (such as copying, postage or foreign mailings), how she plans on being compensated (will she bill you or deduct from revenues?) and whether there is a cap on these expenses.

Other areas that will be covered in the agency agreement are how the contract can be terminated and how disputes between you and your agent can be settled. There will be a clause in this contract about how you authorize the publisher to pay your money directly to your agent and how your agent will pay you. There will also be a clause indemnifying your agent from any legal disputes or misrepresentations to the publisher on your part. This covers your agent against being a third party in a lawsuit from anything from copyright infringement to plagarism.

You can also expect to see a clause, or at least a line, about how you will work with the agent exclusively for the term of the contract or for the submission of the book. What this means is that you can't have two agents at the same time. This should be self-explanatory, but my partner briefly took on a writer who failed to tell him that another agent was sending out the same work simultaneously to the same editors. This is just not done, because there are only a handful of editors who buy certain types of books. As an example of what a small world publishing is, it was the editor who called the two agents to tell them that he had the same proposal from both of them. The writer lost both agents—and the editor didn't buy the book either.

Granting your agent the exclusive right to represent your work also means that you have a moral obligation to tell her if you plan to send out a project that does not fall into her area of expertise (a book of poetry, a script or a comic book). Never assume that she does not want to represent you on something: Ask first. Although there are many areas my agency does not work in, we do have colleagues in these fields, and will often team up with them for representation such as radio anchoring or commercial voice-overs.

My experience with agency contracts is that there is no way to keep an author who wants to leave and no way to force someone who no longer wishes to be your agent to represent you. Yes, on big contracts we can all bring in the lawyers, but it will cost as much, if not more, to untangle a bad situation once lawyers are involved, which is why I choose not to have an agency agreement. I simply include an agency clause in the book publishing contract (which all agents do) stating that I am the agent of record for the book, that all revenue from the book comes through my office, that I promise to pay the author his share of revenues in a timely fashion and that the author has indemnified my agency against misrepresentation. That clause does everything an agency agreement does, without the pages of type. (See chapter four for an example of our agency clause.)

Here are a few red flags to look out for when signing an agency agreement.

• An agreement that ties your current book to the option book in the contract. This language means that you can't leave the agent for two books, which could be quite a few years.

• A nonrefundable handling charge per book, whether or not the agent sells your work. This usually appears as a $50 to $200 charge for handling of the book, which is like a reading fee, so be wary.

• A clause that says that the agent receives her commission on all revenue you make from writing during the term of the contract, whether or not she has helped in the sale. Even if you sell an article yourself, you should tell your agent about it and ask her to negotiate the deal and look over the contract. However, if you choose not to, she should not expect you to send her a check.

If you have questions about the agency agreement, call your agent to discuss them. The best way to do this is to call and leave a message or to send a brief fax saying that you'd like to go over the agreement when she has time. This way you don't waylay her in the middle of an auction. Most agents are willing to negotiate their agreements—within reason. Beware of those agents who say it is a take-it-or-leave-it situation or of those who don't have the time to hear your concerns.

However, there is one area that is non-negotiable, and that is the agency commission. Do not try to be cheap with your agent. You get what you pay for. Your agent should charge the same commission to all her clients. You shouldn't want to be represented by someone who has a different set of fees for each client. If you really want a lower commission, target one of the 10 percent agents.

Once you have signed an agency agreement or have a verbal deal with an agent, you should find out how she will be sending out the material. Most agents will send out three copies of your novel or ten copies of your proposal to the major houses (which is all you really need to know, although she should be willing to tell you which houses they are if you feel you *really* need to know). Once your book project is in the mail, the next thing you will do is wait.

Your agent will always call you as soon as she has remotely positive news, so there is no need to sit by the phone. She will call if an editor has expressed interest in the book, or if an editor has suggestions for improving the material. Rest assured that as soon as a copy of your book returns to her office, she will send it out again. However, it can take anywhere from two weeks to a month before she has genuine feedback to share with you.

If you haven't heard from your agent in a while, feel free to call or E-mail with a request to touch base. I try to return client phone calls within twenty-four hours (as all good agents should). However, it occasionally takes forty-eight hours because of all the meetings we have with editors and authors.

When I was a new agent, I used to send my clients a batch of copies of their rejection letters with a note along the lines of "Here are your rejection letters, but don't be discouraged because I still believe in the book." One of my clients called after receiving such a package and told me that he was so depressed after reading ten editors' reasons for turning down his book that he never wanted me to submit it again. I have since learned to choose which letters I send on to my clients.

If a client asks to see all of his rejection letters, I'll certainly send them on, but, as a published author myself, I can tell you that reading them all doesn't make you a better writer, just a bitter one. Also, if you write a certain kind of book (new age, horror, etc.), your work will always be sent to the same group of editors, many of whom stay in these jobs for decades. You don't want to have a grudge against a certain editor who you may be working with in the future.

As an agent, I always let the editors who turned down a book know where I finally placed it. Remember that agents hate rejection too.

The average nonfiction book sells in two months, and the average novel sells within six months. That does not mean that your work is unsalable if your agent does not have a deal by then. What it means is that the book is not typical to the market it is being sold to, and that your agent now has to find the right editor, which could take a long time.

I went to college with someone who was incredibly talented. After his mother, I think I had been reading his work longer than anyone else. So when I became an agent, I asked to represent him. This is not a good idea (agents should not represent friends or family members—if you have a friend or family member in the business, ask them to recommend a colleague). His novel was brilliantly written when it came to language—every sentence was rich and nuanced—but there were some real problems with plot. I sent the book out anyway. It was rejected by twenty-three editors, which took two and a half years. The editor who finally bought it knew exactly how to fill the plot holes, and the book was published to stellar reviews.

Not every agent is going to send your book to twenty-three editors over two and a half years, but if you have someone who believes in your work, she will get your book out there. Sometimes the market for your kind of book just dries up, but if you have an agent who believes in you, she'll eventually sell it—or help you write something that will sell the next time.

Right now there is a real bust in the horror market, but my heart belongs to horror. Many of my horror authors are making their living writing young adult horror or dark fantasy, but they have a few completed horror novels moldering in their desk drawers. There is one small publisher who has recently started publishing horror again, so my partner and I sold half a dozen trunk novels that had been off the market for years.

What should you do while your agent tries to sell your book? You should be thinking about your next one. You should be doing research, plotting the outline and educating yourself about the publishing industry (more on this in chapter eleven). If you haven't already joined a professional writer's organization, now is the time. You should also be meeting other writers and developing relationships with them so you can get a feel for how the marketplace for your kind of book is doing, and perhaps get some published authors to agree to read your manuscript once you have a publisher.

Once your agent has sold your first book, you should have a conversation about what the both of you think you should be working on next. Do not have this conversation while your first book is unsold: Many agents don't want to work on two books by the same author at the same time. Often, what your next book is depends on the sale (or the lack thereof) of the first.

Many of my authors can work on two tracks in publishing simultaneously because they were trained as journalists and have taught themselves to write fiction. However, I always want to make sure they can meet the first book's deadline before I set them up for another sale. The worst thing you can do for your career is to start out with too much on your plate and get a reputation for missing deadlines.

What I ask my two-track authors to do is to let me know what their priorities are. Are they more concerned with selling fiction or nonfiction, or do they just want me to get them as many contracts as possible so that they can pay their mortgage or buy that new computer? You *must* let your agent know where you are coming from.

These conversations about the shape of your career are really important and should not be sprung on your agent. You should call or E-mail ahead of time, tell him that you'd like to have a conversation about where your career is headed and ask him when it would be a good time to call. If you have his undivided attention, you'll get much better results.

I actually make appointments with my clients to go over their career goals. We do this about two times a year, and sometimes more often for more prolific writers. If one of my clients lives out of town but we regularly attend a convention together, we do this career planning session over an annual meal. I do need to prepare for these sessions so I can give some thought to my client's career and the direction his area of publishing is headed.

Never assume that your agent will set up this career planning discussion. Ultimately, your writing is *your* writing career, and *you* must take responsibility for it.

CHAPTER TEN

How to Keep an Agent Interested in You

Writer-Agent Etiquette

OK, so you've got an agent. Someone's either agreed to send out your work, is sending out your book or has already sold your book. Just because you have an agent, and even a signed agency agreement, doesn't mean that you can't be given a pink slip. The agent/writer relationship is a two-way street, and you always have to be aware of the traffiic on either side. What this means is that you should always be working on and evaluating this relationship, and never forget that you are the driver. Your agent is your navigator.

I will give you a basic list of dos and don'ts for keeping your agent happy, and tell you a few horribly amusing stories about authors I no longer represent and why. But the real gist of this chapter (and all the chapters in this book) is that you are ultimately responsible for the state of your writing career. Although your career is important to your agent's reputation, you have to remember that your agent represents other writers as well.

SILENCE CAN BE GOLDEN

I shouldn't need to tell you that no matter how well you and your agent get along (you love the same movies, are astrologically in synch and have the same middle name), this is a professional relationship. You must refrain from considering your agent a friend who you can call at all hours to discuss this morning's installment of *Donny & Marie*. Your agent is your writing champion and your book's personal advocate, but she is also a working professional who has to juggle the concerns of many writers at the same time, plus have a personal life.

I've been an agent for fifteen years now, and looking back over my career, I cannot think of one legitimate reason why an author should have called me at home. (I can, however, think of many instances where a writer couldn't refrain from tracking me down after hours. Needless to say, I no longer represent most of those authors.) I did (jokingly) tell one author that the only reason he should ever try to reach me at home was if he received a quote from Stephen King and could not contain his excitement, and, lo and behold, he got a quote from King on a Sunday and just had to call me. But even that could have waited until the next business day—or he could have faxed me.

Although this is the brave new technological world of faxes, E-mail, voice mail and cell phones, there is absolutely no reason why you should feel you need to call your agent (or your editor) at home unless they ask you to do so. Even if they're working from home one day and give you their home number, you should not consider it an open invitation to call there again.

After I had my son, I worked from home for five years. I had a completely separate office and phone lines, but many authors called at night and over the weekend just to see if I might be working. I had one author who called on Christmas Eve with a panic attack, which my entire family heard blaring from the answering machine. ("Are you really going to sell my book and exactly how soon will that be and for how much?") I promptly severed that relationship.

Another author overstepped her boundaries when I gave birth. I notified all my clients of my child's imminent arrival and took a week to recover from the birth. I told my clients I would be processing checks and contracts, but I wouldn't be doing any active business for about ten days. My son was born over Labor Day, so there was no pressing business pending in the book world. I left a message on the answering machine when I went into labor, which unfortunately for me and my clients was a three-day ordeal. One of my clients just couldn't wait and left a tirade on my machine about when I was going to send him his $50 royalty check. Needless to say, I no longer represent him.

You should treat your agent's time with respect and realize that she keeps office hours that are basically Monday through Friday, 9:00 A.M. to 5:00 P.M. or 10:00 A.M. to 6:00 P.M. Some agents take Friday as a reading day. Anything that happens during nonoffice hours should be handled by fax, E-mail or voice mail.

It is never a good idea to call your agent with a panic attack. What I recommend to my authors—some of whom I've walked through one of these crises—is that they take a deep breath, write it all down and either fax me or E-mail me. If I'm working after hours or checking voice mail (which I do regularly), I will usually send them a "Don't worry" note with assurances that we'll take care of this catastrophe on the next business day.

Most of the time, when we speak the next morning, the author realizes that this incident didn't even register on the Richter Scale and we can deal with whatever the situation presents. Publishing is an extremely slow medium, and nothing ever happens overnight.

WHEN TO TALK

That's not to say that your agent doesn't care or that she doesn't want to hear about whatever is bothering you. You should never hold back from telling your agent what's on your mind. If some personal matter is distracting you, call your agent at a time when you know she has more time to talk and tell her what's going on. Don't surprise her afterward and say you missed your deadline because your mother died, when you didn't even tell her that your mother was ill. Your agent will be able to get you an extension on your deadline from your editor before you miss your deadline, which will give you time to catch your breath—and keep your relationship with your editor on sound ground.

Any editorially related issues should be brought up to your agent as soon as they surface. If you are having a conflict with your editor, tell your agent. You should always copy your agent on all your correspondence with your editor, so that she can see how things are going. Sometimes a new author misses some of the editorial euphemisms that mean a book is in trouble, but your agent will catch them. Sometimes your editor is way off base, and your agent can gently guide the editor back. Sometimes your agent has to go over your editor's head. You and she should discuss all these things together.

When you're under contract, don't send each chapter of your book to your agent as you write it, but do drop her some kind of note to let her know how you're progressing. If you think you might miss your deadline, let your agent know first. Don't try to handle this on your own.

Some writers think that once the agent has sold the book her work is done—until they get into some kind of trouble. Often, a writer grows very close to his editor because they are watching his "baby" grow together, and they often leave the agent out of the loop. This is a very bad decision, because your agent will be looking at the whole picture of publishing your book, not just getting it to production. While your editor may love the book, she may not have the clout or sales ability to get the most from publicity, or she may not want to tell the art department that the cover stinks, but your agent will.

You can also play good cop/bad cop with your editor, using your agent as the bad cop. If you don't like something and are getting the editorial runaround when you bring it up to your editor, a phone call or a letter from your agent will let your editor know just how serious the situation is.

One client I've been working with for years requested that I send a book to an editor he considered a friend. I told him that that editor was not my first choice at that house, but if he really wanted me to send it to him, I would. He bought the book and made promises that were heart-poundingly good. Months later, the friend/editor called me when the book was delivered to tell me that it was unpublishable and that I should tell the author because *he* was the author's friend.

I had no idea that the author was having these kind of problems with the book. I did know that the editor had taken an incredibly long time to get back to us with his comments, so I asked to see the manuscript, and he was right. It was unpublishable, not because the author had written a bad book, but because the first two chapters were all wrong. The editorial work that needed to be done was so simple a college English major could have made the changes. I called the editor's boss and told her my thoughts. She had read the manuscript and had wondered how it had been sent to her in such a state. I wondered too. We all had a meeting and the book was edited. It was published in hardcover the next year.

Personal problems are another issue. You should always let your agent know what is going on in your life, but you shouldn't tell your editor everything unless you know she's experienced the same thing (a difficult pregnancy, family illness or a horrendous divorce). It might be easier for you if you let your agent handle bringing up really dicey matters such as divorce or money problems. Keep in mind that this is a professional relationship, so your agent doesn't need to know the details of how you found the lipstick-stained collar and receipts from the hotel room.

If you are having money problems, you have to let your agent know. It could affect your career in ways you can't imagine. One of my clients was invited to appear on CNN on Halloween (a great coup for us), and the publisher had made arrangements to have a car pick him up and take him to the airport and then drive him to the studio. Unfortunately he was writing under a pseudonym, and the driver was looking for someone else when he got off the plane. He didn't want to tell me that he was absolutely broke, so he waited an hour in the airport and then used a credit card to take a cab, but it was too late. They had filmed the segment without him. If he had only told me he was out of money, I would have advanced him some for this important opportunity.

Another author was well published but, as a result of a difficult divorce, became very concerned about money. Instead of
bringing the topic up with her agent, she decided to take
matters into her own hands. Having met some editors years
ago, before she had an agent, she proceeded to submit material
that she didn't think her agent would be interested in sending
out to an editor who had died and another editor who had
gone through such a dreadful divorce herself that she told
everyone she knew that she would not even read a proposal
addressed to her former married name. Thankfully, this editor
called the agent and said something along the lines of "What
the hell is your client doing sending this stuff directly to me
when you're the agent, and didn't I tell you to stop using that
last name?"

When the agent had a long talk with his client about how
things are done in publishing, she said she understood, but
every once in a while the author gets a mad urge to be her
own agent and send something directly to an editor. At least
now she tells the agent first, and he can usually talk her out
of it.

Panic over finances and personal problems conspires to
make writers do things that can be dangerous to their careers,
or just foolish, and without someone on the outside to tell
them that something is not a good idea, they often insert their
foot directly in their mouths. One author decided to come to
New York to meet her editors (she had multiple book deals)
and see if she could get one or two additional commitments
in the process. She had written one nonfiction book proposal
with her new boyfriend, but most of her work was in a completely different field. However, she wanted the new boyfriend to accompany her to all her editorial meetings. It took
quite a lot of convincing to talk her out of her escort (we
promised to be there for every meeting), and she said she
understood. Two days later, she called to ask me if her teenage
son could come to the breakfast meeting we were having to
discuss her career. Through clinched teeth, I tried to explain
that I did not think it was a good idea for her son to hear us

discussing the possibilities of her career, which she had a hard time understanding until I pointed out to her that she might not want him to know she was interested in writing erotica or exactly how much she made per book.

Once your first book is finished, you and your agent should discuss the next book. This is the time for you to tell your agent where you want to go with your career and how you hope your career will progress. You should feel comfortable about brainstorming with your agent, but you should also take her advice if she tells you that horror isn't selling right now, or that it's not a good idea to work on that short story collection at this point in your career.

Do not discuss your next book with your editor first, or she will think that she already has a lock on the next book (even though she does have the option and will most likely buy the next book) and will try to lowball you on the next offer. Never, under any circumstances, talk money with your editor: This is what you have an agent for.

My business partner tells an amusing story about an author who came to him when he was an editor at Walker and Company. The author had been published very well at other houses, but had been out of contract for some years. In desperation, he sent his book out on his own, and my partner made him a relatively small offer for world rights. A few days later his agent called to talk about the offer, which was a surprise to my partner. She was a well-respected agent. She calmly explained to my partner that the author had not been well while sending out his book, which had caused him to agree to the terms on the table. My partner had no other recourse than to improve the deal if he wanted to publish the book.

Although editors love books and like authors, they don't work for them. They work for the publisher. They will never give you the best terms for your book without someone intervening on your behalf. They will not love you any more if you let them take advantage of you. So always remember why you have an agent: to look out for your business interests.

AGENT ETIQUETTE DOS AND DON'TS

I have a long list of things my authors do that make me happy to be their agent, and an even longer list of things they do that drive me to drink way too much coffee. Here are my top five contenders.

The Dos

1. Surprise me and say thank you. It doesn't matter how authors do it—by E-mail, with a phone message, with a card, with flowers or even with a comic book—but it's nice to get an acknowledgment for the work you've done. It's especially appreciated on a really rotten day. It's also really nice to get some kind of acknowledgment in the published book.

2. Keep me posted. You'd be surprised at how many authors have wonderful career moments that they forget to tell me about. Call or E-mail me about your invitation to speak at the Smithsonian, or send me the news clip of your interview in the local paper. Just because that book's already published doesn't mean that I can't do something with the publicity or that it's not of interest to me.

3. Help me. Get those quotes, call the local paper to set up an interview and send me a written list of your foreign publishers so I can send it on to my foreign agents. Don't make me track everything down myself, if you can help it. It's great when my authors are mindful of my workload and try to make things just that much easier for me.

4. Be honest. Tell me right away that you don't want to write a book, that you don't care about the size of the advance because you have always wanted to write a *Star Trek* novel or that the only thing you care about is getting as much money as possible by April 15.

5. Learn about the industry. Educate yourself about how the publishing industry works, as well as what's selling. If you're reading about what's selling and what's not, you'll have a good idea of what your next project should—or shouldn't—be.

The Don'ts

1. Don't overwhelm me. This relates to everything from sending me too many projects to calling too often, to even wanting too much editorial handholding. Once you are my client, I will do everything I can to make you feel special and well cared for.

2. Don't second guess me. I hate this. I want to sell your book for as much money as possible as badly as you do, so if things don't seem to be moving as quickly as we thought or for as much as we thought, just accept that that's what the market will bear.

3. Don't kill the messenger. No one likes to be the bearer of bad news, but occasionally an agent has to give up on a project or accept that the only offer out there is far less than what she expected. The worst thing you can do is blame your agent.

4. Don't harass me about money, contracts or deals. I don't get paid until you get paid, so rest assured that I am tracking your money as carefully as you are. The same goes for the contracts. As far as getting your deals is concerned, there's no guarantee when material goes on submission, but added pressure from the author rarely helps an agent consummate a deal quicker.

5. Don't argue with me. My job in your life is to sell your work, so if I think you need to do more work on your book or proposal, I'm asking you to do the work so we can sell your book.

PART III

THE SALE

CHAPTER ELEVEN

HELPING YOUR AGENT BY HELPING YOURSELF

It's Your Writing Career, After All

Just because you have an agent, an editor and a publisher doesn't mean you're going to make it to the best-seller list. The difference between Dean Koontz and some unknown genre novelist is not only talent, but also hard work on the part of the author.

THE DEAN KOONTZ STORY (FROM MY POINT OF VIEW)

Dean Koontz has been publishing novels since his early twenties, and he's in his early fifties now, but he didn't make the best-seller lists until he had been publishing for twenty years. He published his first short story when he was in his teens and began writing way before that.

Koontz always knew he wanted to be a writer, although he was a teacher in his young-adult years to pay the bills. Once he began to sell his novels on a consistent basis, he quit his day job and wrote furiously (at least four, if not eight, novels a year) to match the meager living he was making as a teacher. After publishing in genre fiction for a few years and not really moving up, he decided to reevaluate his career and write *better* books instead of *more* books. He educated himself about the publishing industry, saw what was selling well and re-created himself as a writer. He stopped writing so many books a year and moved away from genre writing and into thrillers.

When he became dissatisfied with something in his career, he researched it and then set a course to correct it. Case in point: his foreign sales. Koontz felt his publisher was not working as hard as he could to sell his books in foreign countries, so he took back all his foreign rights, and he and his wife sold them themselves for years.

Koontz always had a vision for himself and was willing to work extremely hard, yet be flexible and teach himself new things to succeed (such as selling in foreign markets). He has always been a giving part of the writing community, constantly giving advice to novice writers (and young agents) who would seek him out. He knew that writing was a profession just like any other, and in order to succeed and get to the top, he had to be disciplined. He worked at least eight hours a day, seven days a week, with no vacations for years, and still finds it hard to take time off from his writing. Even before computers became so inexpensive, he rewrote and polished his novels at least twenty times, and sometimes more.

Dean Koontz made it to the top of the best-seller lists because he worked hard. Even though he was born with an innate storytelling ability, he worked on his craft and his career constantly. It was the combination of hard work, talent and a little bit of luck (being in the right place at the right time and finding the right editor at a house that saw his vision) that have made him what he is today.

WHAT YOU CAN DO

Just as in the art and music worlds, there's a lot of talent out there. Some people are born gifted, but most of us have to hone our craft. The same goes for writing.

One of my friends who is a novelist once complained that all these no-talent writers were getting huge advances, great publicity and making the best-seller lists, while he had more talent in his pinky and his novels seemed to be going nowhere right off of the printing press. He blamed his publisher, their publicist, his editor and his agent. He changed publishers, editors and agents, and still nothing happened. It never dawned on him to take a good look at himself.

Successful authors today must expect to do much more for

their careers than just write books. You don't have to sell them (that is what your agent is for), but you have to learn about the publishing industry and learn to sell yourself—to your editor, to your publisher, to other writers and to your readers.

How do you do this? It's actually easier than you think.

Educate Yourself About the Publishing Industry

To learn about the publishing industry, once you have a book contract, subscribe to *Publisher's Weekly*, the magazine that chronicles the events and trends of the publishing industry. It may be a bit pricey (I believe it currently runs about $170 a year), but it's worth it—and a tax deduction to boot. Read it religiously, not just to see how much other authors are getting for their books, but also to see what editors and agents are saying about the changing industry.

Make it a point to read your newspaper's weekly book review, as well as national newspaper columns about book publishing (you should be able to find most of these articles on the Internet). You should also start reading the business sections of the papers for publishing company mergers and what they mean to you, as well as the gossip pages for news of the latest teenage rock star's multimillion dollar sale of her autobiographical poetry.

Join a Writers Organization

You need to be able to talk to other people about these trends in publishing, and your editor is not the best person to do this with because she has her publishing company's interests at heart. You should be able to talk to your agent about these issues, but she won't be able to give you the kind of daily gossip you really need (she's too busy selling—and gossiping with other agents). The best people to talk shop with are other writer's, and you do this by joining professional writers organizations. Again, the annual membership fees are tax deductible.

Every kind of writer has an organization he can belong to, whether he's a children's book writer, a science writer, a literary novelist or a journalist. There are umbrella writer's organizations such as The Author's Guild, the Writer's Union and the American Society of Journalists and Authors, as well as specific writer's organizations by genre and type of book. Depending on where you live and how social you are, you might even want to join two organizations—a general one and the one for your genre—because they all have meetings. Many cities also have regional writers organizations.

These organizations usually publish a monthly newsletter and distribute a membership list. Many have Web sites where you can look through back issues of the newsletter and various archives. They also have chat areas for writers.

I know that when I was a new agent it was important for me to meet other new agents, especially those who sold the same kind of books as I did. We gossiped, had dinner, exchanged information on editors and advances and problem contract negotiations and gave each other support. Writers need to do the same thing for each other. They understand the ups and downs of the industry from your perspective better than anyone else, including your spouse.

Go to a Writers Convention

It's an "I'll scratch your back if you'll scratch my back" kind of business, so it's important to be in the backscratching circle. The more established writers will often read your book to give you feedback, and perhaps even give you a quote, especially if you've corresponded with them over the months of writing your book or you've met them at the annual convention of the writer's organization. This is how those young first novelists come bursting out of the publishing gates with quotes from best-selling authors.

Although your agent may represent a few best-sellers herself, it's not her job to get you quotes. Also, it's easier for a successful author to turn down his agent's request for a favor for an author he doesn't know ("I've got to finish this book") than it is for him to turn down a writer he's been mentoring. Don't ever forget to thank someone who has taken the time to give you a quote, even if the publisher doesn't use it or you don't think it's good enough.

Writers conventions are also important to a new writer because you get to see your area of publishing set apart from the rest of the book world. You get to meet prominent authors in your field, as well as the editors who buy your kind of books. You get invited into anthologies this way and become part of the "in" group. You hear about sideline writing gigs (computer games or comic books), and when it comes time for award nominations, the nominating committee knows who you are. At the beginning of a writer's career, these contacts are invaluable (and the convention trip is also tax deductible).

Book Expo America
Every year, around Memorial Day, the publishing industry holds its annual convention called Book Expo America (BEA— once called the ABA, after the American Booksellers Association, which sponsored it). It's usually in a fairly interesting city (Los Angeles, Chicago, Miami, Las Vegas, Washington D.C. and New Orleans are some of the recent locations), so it can double as a family vacation—and still be partly tax deductible.

If you are at all serious about writing (even if it's a hobby and you never plan on leaving your day job), you should attend this convention at least once. It will give you an overview of the coming year in publishing that will make your head spin.

What you will see there are rows upon rows upon rows of books being presented to bookstore buyers by all the publishers in the United States, and some foreign publishers as well. Almost all the major publishers (except one or two who boycott because of lawsuits or on the principle that the convention costs too much) and all the small and academic presses, as well as a few hundred self-publishers, display their titles for the coming year. Publishers give away advance reading copies of books (called ARCs in the trade), posters, bookmarks, buttons and all sorts of marketing-related gizmos to call attention to their titles in this dizzying array of nearly 50,000 different books coming to bookstores in the next calendar year. It will inspire awe in you and will also make you very aware of the competition you face every day.

It should also inspire you to want to become one of those authors whose publishing company features them prominently at their booth for signings, readings and breakfasts with the media. The way to become one of those writers is to write the best damn book you can, finding out how everyone before you did it and then improving on their success.

My authors and I brainstorm constantly. They tell me their dreams, I give them a dose of reality, and then we come up with a plan to get them there. It's usually a ten-year plan. I can't guarantee overnight success—or I'd be on that best-seller list myself.

Read

I can always tell a real amateur by a writer telling me he never reads other writers' books or that he only reads the classics. How can you possibly know what the marketplace is like if you don't know what's on the best-seller list and why it got there?

You should be familiar with the work of every writer on the best-seller list, even if they are writing in a genre you can't stomach. You don't have to read the whole book, but you should have read some of the writing by what I call the usual suspects (those who make the best-seller lists regularly), which include Stephen King, Dean Koontz, Anne Rice, Mary Higgins Clark, Danielle Steele, Tom Clancy, Jonathan Kellerman, Michael Crichton and John Grisham. In addition, you should read the books that make surprise appearances on the best-seller lists, especially first novels such as *Cold Mountain* by Charles Frazier or oddball books like *Midnight in the Garden of Good and Evil* by John Berendt.

Work on Your Craft

There's one more thing you can do to advance your writing career aside from educating yourself about the industry, joining organizations and getting quotes, and that's working on your craft as a writer. That means everything from taking a refresher course on grammar (if your manuscript came back from your editor with too many grammatical mistakes) to reading books on editing and writing, to taking writing classes where you can work on your weakest writing areas.

For the unpublished or newly published author, I strongly recommend joining a writer's workshop. These can be anything from an established group of students from a fiction writing class, to a class offered through a university or community center (like a Y), to a local group of writers who come together to review each other's work. Most writers workshops are free, but some are given as a class with a published writer running things, so you pay for the guidance and the space rental.

When I was a young writer, I answered an ad in *The Village Voice* calling for new members in an established writing group. I submitted a writing sample and was invited to join. The group was made up of both published and unpublished writers of both fiction and nonfiction. It was a constant inspiration to me, as well as a deadline, although some of the members were unbelievably pompous. One young man who lived on a trust fund asked me how many hours I wrote a day, as if the amount of time you wrote was the true sign of a real writer.

When I began publishing my newspaper I had no time to travel downtown for a writer's group, but I still wanted the feedback and inspiration, so I put an ad in my own newspaper and formed a writer's workshop in my neighborhood. I asked people to submit works in progress, and anyone who seemed committed to working on their writing was invited in. We met weekly, first at the newspaper offices after hours and then, after I sold the paper, at each other's homes, rotating meeting places every week. Each week, two authors read about ten pages (or a chapter of a work in progress) and we gave our reaction. Of the six regular members of that group four are published, and four of us became literary agents.

This is a great point to tell you the story of one of my favorite clients, because it should be a real inspiration to anyone who really wants to get published well. I took him on when he was in his late thirties. He worked in the publishing industry, so he already knew most of the people I was just meeting. He had self-published his first novel (a limited edition for all his friends in publishing), and I read it to see if there was a way I could sell it to a major house. The writing was awful, but he had a gift for character, dialogue, setting and storytelling. I finished the book, turning page after page in spite of my urge to grab a red pencil as I read. I didn't know what to tell him, because he was a friend of everyone I wanted to know.

I sold his book to one of the smallest houses, who paid him a very meager advance. He was elated. Finally he was a published author, and now he wanted to move on to the bigger houses. I wrestled with what I should tell him, but finally decided on the truth and told him that I could never sell his work to a major publisher if he didn't work on his writing skills. I sent him Strunk and White's *Elements of Style* and even told him to think about taking a night class at the local high school to brush up on his grammar. I was certain I'd never hear from him again.

About six months later, he called me to tell me he was sending me three chapters and the outline of his next book, and that he wanted to thank me for suggesting he get some help with his writing. I dreaded reading what he was about to send me, but when it came in, it was fabulous. All the talent and brilliance I had seen in the earlier novel was still there, but this time the writing was seamless. I was thrilled and sold the book for ten times what we had received for the first novel.

I've been representing this author for nearly fifteen years now. We've sold thirteen novels and two nonfiction books together, and his two most recent books are hardcovers that have a shot at the best-seller lists. We've had our ups and downs, but we're a team, and I've always appreciated the hard work he puts into each book.

CHAPTER TWELVE

THE FIRST SALE

Deal-Making, Contracts and
Waiting for Checks

Your agent has been sending your material out for two weeks (or two years), when suddenly you receive a call that says there's good news. This is what you've been waiting for your whole life!

Your agent will most likely tell you that she has an offer to publish your book. She will then tell you what rights the publisher would like to buy and whether she thinks this is a good offer. She may also tell you how she hopes to improve the offer and what her strategy for doing that will be.

If your work is still being reviewed by other editors, she will now call all of them and let them know that there is an offer on the table. This will get them to read the material quickly and let her know if they have any interest in pursuing it. An offer on the table makes everyone work faster. What once took two weeks now takes twenty-four or forty-eight hours.

An offer on the table is not magic. Sometimes the other editors just can't work as quickly as your agent needs them to, so they pass on the book without giving it a full read—but they will remember that they lost the opportunity if the book does well.

While the other editors are trying to get their acts together, your agent will tell the editor who has made the offer that she has the material out with a few other editors and that she will get back to her as soon as she hears from them. Your agent may immediately try to get the editor to improve the offer by saying that it is too low or that she will not sell foreign rights. That editor will then go back to the person holding the purse strings to see if there is any flexibility on the deal.

If the house that made the offer is the only taker, your agent has less room to maneuver. That's why she will start trying to improve the deal before all the other editors have responded. Once an editor knows that there is no other publisher interested in the book (even if it's because they made their offer so quickly and the other houses couldn't move as fast), she will start thinking that she is bidding against herself, and it will be harder for your agent to get her to improve the offer. However, a good agent will still be able to improve the offer, even it's just in the royalty rate.

If you are lucky and more than one editor is interested in publishing your book, you and your agent now have the upper hand. You can play editors off of one another. Your agent can get one house to give up foreign rights and then tell the other that the terms have changed. This back-and-forth, inch-by-inch process can go on for days.

UP FOR AUCTION

If you're really lucky and at least three houses are interested, your agent will probably set an auction date and have them begin bidding on a certain day. The way this is usually done is that an auction letter is faxed to all those who have said that they will be in the auction, setting the time, date and procedure for the bidding.

A typical auction letter from an agent would read:

> Dear Editor:
>
> We will be accepting your best offer for *The Making of Blade Runner* by Paul M. Sammon beginning at 10:00 A.M. on Wednesday, February 3.
>
> Please include any promotional terms you are willing to commit to in your offer.
>
> If there is no clear winner, the auction will continue in rounds, starting with the lowest bidder.

> The author reserves the right to review the entire
> offer, and to make his decision based on all factors.
> We look forward to hearing your bid on
> Wednesday.

Your agent should discuss the terms for the sale of your
book with you, even if you don't really understand what she
is talking about. If you don't understand something, this is the
time to ask questions and make sure it all makes sense to you.

Sometimes the house who called with the first offer will
ask for a *floor* on the book. This means that they will open
the bidding with a preset amount (which is included in the
auction letter) and that they have the right to top the highest
bid by 10 percent. Giving one house the floor often scares
off the other publishers, because you are giving one house a
decided advantage, but sometimes it starts the bidding at a
much higher price.

You and your agent have a right to negotiate the floor before
the auction, because it sets the tone for the auction. Often
publishers ask for a floor and come back with an offer that is
lower than you and your agent expected, considering that you
are weighing whether or not to give them that advantage.
Sometimes you and your agent might decide not to give anybody a floor because you think you have a really hot book and
you want to see what the market will bear.

Sometimes you and your agent set the floor. This usually
happens when the author has a minimum amount in mind for
the book (there are a lot of research or travel expenses, or the
author must take time off from a lucrative job to write the
book), and you want the publishers to know that the author
cannot, or is unwilling to, write the book for less. This is risky,
because publishers do not like being told how much you think
a book is worth.

While good auctions are exciting, many books today are
sold in unnecessary auctions, when two publishers simply
compete against each other without the stress of a big deal.
Every agent has set an auction date and been disappointed

when only one player came to the table (and sometimes no one comes), so setting up an auction isn't a sure thing. Most of the books I sell are sold with gentle negotiation between two publishers. We all remain friendly that way, and no one feels that they lost a book.

I've sold more than a thousand books, but only about fifty of them went to auction. Some of those auctions were furious six-figure deals with five or six publishers, but many were for much smaller books where the increases in the advance went up $1,000 or $2,500 at a time. One auction started with an opening bid of $5,000, had seven publishers involved, and over the course of two days went for $110,000.

If your book is going to auction, your agent might ask you to come to New York to do "the dog-and-pony show." She will set up meetings with the prospective editors, who will also bring their marketing and publicity personnel, so they can see just how witty and photogenic you are when it comes to getting you on *Oprah*. This is grueling work. You have to be as spiffed up as possible—perfect hair, clothes, etc.—and sometimes you will see six different editors in two days.

The other reason a good agent will ask if you will come to New York is so that you can meet the editors who will be bidding on your book. She will want you to get a feel for the personality and vision that each editor, and each house, has for you and the book. Often, at the end of an auction you have two houses with nearly identical bids in terms of the advance, and the author and agent must decide who they want to publish the book. Having met the principals involved gives the author some concrete basis for making this difficult decision, which will set the pace for your future in publishing.

TERMS OF THE SALE

The terms of the deal that your agent will review with you include the following items.

The Advance

Most authors already know about this one. It's the amount of money the publishing company will pay you before the book is published. It is supposed to be based on the profit-and-loss calculations that the editor submits on the book, which are supposed to show how much the house can expect to earn on the book based on sales and subsidiary rights. The full term is *advance against royalties*.

However, most books never *earn out*, which means that their sales and revenue do not pay back the advance. One big book that makes much more than the publisher paid for it can earn enough profit to pay for an entire list of books that don't earn back their advances.

The Payout

This is how the publisher will make payments to the author. Until recently, most authors could expect to be paid half the advance on signing the contract (the *signing payment*) and the remainder on delivery and acceptance of the manuscript (the *D&A payment*). If photos or illustrations are involved, there is often a separate payment for the photo budget, but the author will rarely receive his D&A payment without delivering the complete manuscript, which includes all supporting documents such as photos, illustrations and permissions.

In the past five years, with Harvard MBAs coming in to review publishers' account ledgers and more and more mergers, publishers have taken a much tighter rein on how they pay out money to authors. Every publisher will now try to break up the advance into three payments, with the third payment upon publication of the book. For larger advances (those over $100,000), publishers are even trying to add on a fourth payment upon publication of the paperback edition of the work. In a worst-case scenario, this could mean that the author won't finish receiving the advance until two years after he's delivered the book!

If you must take a publication payment, your agent will add language that states that you will be paid on publication or twelve months after delivery and acceptance of the manuscript, whichever comes first. This protects you from a delay in publishing that would delay your receipt of the remainder of your advance.

The Due Date

This is the date when the completed manuscript is due, complete with photos and illustrations. Most publishers want a computer disk now too. Your agent will discuss the due date with you before the contract is drawn up. It's usually six months to a year after the signing of the contract. However, if the book is already completed (such as a first novel), there might be a shorter due date.

For first books, some houses request that the author send the first half of the manuscript in; a good agent will make a payment coincide with this delivery date.

For books that involve a lot of research, there might be a longer due date (two years, so a half-manuscript payment will come in very handy to the author). For books that are extremely timely, such as popular biographies and movie novelizations, the due date might be as short as six weeks.

The Territories

This covers the countries in which the publisher will have the right to publish your book. The best deal for an author who has an agent is to sell only the rights to publishers in the United States and Canada. Your agent can then have her foreign agents in other countries sell those rights for you. If your agent's foreign agents do sell these rights for you, you will not have to wait for the book to earn out to receive your foreign money, as you would if the publisher sold those rights, because that money is held against the advance.

However, with the international conglomeratization of publishing, more and more houses are insisting on buying foreign rights. They try to buy *World English Rights*, which include the right to publish their edition in the United Kingdom and all the English-speaking countries, as well as the right to sell their edition in English throughout the world. This means that the American edition of the book, as opposed to the British edition, will be the one sold in English-speaking outlets in France and Israel. In the new European market, this makes the British less than happy.

World Rights gives the publisher the right to publish in the United Kingdom and to sell the right to publish your book in translation throughout the world. This could mean as many as twenty different languages (and editions) of the work.

The Royalty Rate

There are three kinds of royalty rates: hardcover, trade paperback and mass market. Each one of them is different.

Hardcover royalties are more or less standard in the publishing industry. Publishers will credit the author's account 10 percent of the first 5,000 copies sold, 12.5 percent of the next 5,000 copies sold, and 15 percent thereafter. For a really big book, your agent might be able to get a higher royalty rate after 15,000 copies sold, which is called an *escalator*.

Trade paperback royalties range from 6 to 7.5 percent. The best houses will give you a flat royalty rate of 7.5 percent to start. Others will start at 6 percent for the first 25,000 copies and then go up to 7 percent for the next 10,000 and 7.5 percent thereafter.

Mass market royalties vary the most. Royalties of 8 and 10 percent were the industry standard a few years ago, but even the best houses will now try to start at 6 percent for the first 150,000 copies sold, go to 8 percent for the next 50,000 or 100,000, and then go up to 10 percent thereafter. You should always try to get 8 percent for the first 150,000 copies sold, and 10 percent thereafter. Your agent may even be able to get an escalator above and beyond the 10 percent.

A few houses will try to start with a 4 percent royalty rate, but you should sign elsewhere if you can, because this will make it that much harder for you to earn out your advance.

The Subsidiary Rights

These are the smaller additional sales that bring in revenue from your book. They include first and second serial rights (newspaper and magazine reprint before and after publication), book club, audio rights, film and dramatic rights, merchandising rights (calendars, T-shirts, comic books and action figures), electronic rights, large print and so on. An author who has an agent who will sell these rights should always retain the dramatic rights and should try to retain the first serial, audio, electronic and merchandising rights, unless the publisher has a strong track record of selling those rights. Publishers usually keep second serial (after book publication) and book club rights.

Publishers are now becoming crazed about keeping electronic rights, even though only a fraction of the books published manage to get electronic deals, and they often say that this will be a deal breaker. If your agent cannot retain those rights, she should set a time limit on how long the publisher has to sell them before they revert back to the author.

The Option

This can be a killer clause for the uninitiated author. Its purpose is to give the publisher who has invested in you a first look at, and first chance to buy, your next book, but publishers often get greedy and try to buy the right to your next book *and* your right arm.

The option clause should be limited to a thirty-day first look at the outline and three chapters of your next novel, or the proposal for your nonfiction book. However, some publishers will ask to see the next book you write (whether it's fiction or nonfiction) and, if you don't sell that, the next book after that. Some publishers will try to insert a "topping" clause that gives them the right to outbid another publisher by paying 10 percent more than their offer. The topping privilege is onerous in that it discourages other publishers from making a bid because they know that someone else has the right to take the book away for 10 percent more.

The Extras

Your agent might try to build some extras into the contract if she thinks the book has a shot at the best-seller list. The most obvious extras are royalty escalators and best-seller bonuses. Every house has a standard best-seller bonus package where they will give the author extra money for each week the book places on certain best-seller lists (usually *The New York Times* or *Publisher's Weekly*), up to a maximum of ten, twenty-five or even fifty-two weeks.

A best-seller bonus clause looks something like this:

> For each week the book places number fifteen through eleven on *The New York Times* best-seller list, the publisher will pay the author $1,000, up to a maximum of twenty-five weeks.
>
> For each week the book places number ten through five, the publisher will pay the author $2,500, for a maximum of twenty-five weeks.
>
> For each week the book places number four through two, the publisher will give the author $5,000, up to a maximum of twenty-five weeks.
>
> For each week that the book places number one on the best-seller list, the publisher will give the author $10,000 for a maximum of twenty-five weeks.

Your agent will also ask for author consultation on the book cover and jacket copy. This is not so you can design the book cover (of the thousand books I've sold, only one publisher used the cover illustration the author's friend drew up), but so that the publisher will send you the jacket early enough for you to catch stupid errors, such as the misspelling of your name, mistaken credentials or *really* bad jacket copy.

The contract usually gives the author ten to twenty-five free copies of each edition of the book. We ask that an additional ten copies be sent to the agent. Occasionally the author can get as many as fifty free copies. If a book is truly publicity driven and the author has fabulous contacts, the publisher may give him as many as one hundred copies. However, all publishers give the author the right to purchase copies at a deep discount (usually 40 to 60 percent off) that they can charge against their royalty account (which means the author doesn't have to pay for them out of pocket).

Your agent will also add a *First Proceeds* clause if one does not already exist in the contract. This is language that states that should the publisher turn down the book once it is delivered, you have a year to resell the book, and any money advanced to you will be paid out of first proceeds of another sale. This is insurance language, so that if a publisher capriciously changes editorial direction, they can't expect you to repay an advance at the drop of a hat. However, you do have to make an attempt to resell the book.

Publishers have a handful of little extras they like to sneak into a contract as well. The most egregious of these is the *joint accounting* or *basketing* clause, wherein they consider multiple books as one book (three books at $10,000 each are now considered one that has to earn out $30,000) and therefore hold the entire advance for two or three books against sales, which means it could take forever for your books to earn out. This would mean that even if your first book in a three-book $30,000 contract earns $12,000, you won't see royalties on it until the third book has been published, which could be as long as three years after the first book was published. That's a long time to wait for money that you've earned.

BEFORE YOU SIGN

Once the terms for the sale of your book are in place, you and your agent will wait for the contract. On average, this takes six to eight weeks, and sometimes longer during the summer (when people tend to go on vacation) and during the Thanksgiving through New Year's season (when people take off for the holidays).

Your agent should have a *boilerplate contract* with each publishing house, which means that she has already reviewed that house's contract and has struck out the most author-unfriendly clauses—or at least improved them. Each house has its own little "private hell" clauses for writers, but a good agent should already know what these are and how to fix them. The contract that is sent on to you through your agent will already contain these improvements.

You don't need to hire a lawyer to go over your contract for the average book deal. Save the money and hire a publicist when your book is published (see chapter fourteen on publicity).

Many first-time authors have a family friend or a friend of a friend who is a lawyer who they ask to review the contract. If the lawyer is not familiar with publishing, or at least entertainment law, your agent will spend hours teaching him about publishing contracts. While I like lawyers, I have never been able to substantially improve a contract after a family-friend lawyer has reviewed it. Most of the things they ask to improve have been prenegotiated in the deal-making process (such as the advance, payout and royalty rate). However, I have learned an awful lot about improving contract clauses from established writers, other agents, editors who tell me their companies' contract clause secrets, and contract managers.

If you have any questions about the contract, have your agent explain things to you. If you have special concerns, your agent will probably be able to come up with language that will cover it. While publishers and agents are adversaries on behalf of the writer, we have to work with each other all the time and can usually work something out.

GETTING PAID

Once you and your agent have reviewed the contract, you will be asked to initial all changes and sign on the dotted line. The contract will be sent back to the publisher, who will sign it and then send it to the accounting department to draw up your signing payment. This also takes about six to eight weeks. Many authors finish the book in the time it takes to get the contract and signing payment.

All author payments are sent to the agent. This is the standard practice in the industry, so do not ask if the publisher will send you the check or your portion of the check. This practice makes it easier for accounting purposes and ensures that your agent gets paid. Your agent will usually pay you within ten days of receipt. Most agents will let you know when the check comes in, and they will bug the publisher for you if it is late (that's another service an agent provides).

However, as soon as you and your agent have agreed to the terms of the deal, you should begin working on your book. For the first-time author, there are often surprises along the way about how hard it is to work a day job and write at night or how long it will take to finish the book. The sooner you get started, the sooner you will get that D&A payment.

CHAPTER THIRTEEN

WRITING THE FIRST BOOK

Or, This Isn't as Easy as You Thought

Now that I've written a book myself, I can honestly say that no one in the publishing industry could possibly understand what it takes to write a book until they've done it. I now believe that everyone who works in publishing should write a book, edit a book and sell a book, so that we can truly appreciate each other's jobs.

Before I wrote my first book, I had always thought of writing as this wonderful hobby and talent that I had that gave me great pleasure, and sometimes earned me a little bit of money (mostly for articles). I thought writing a book would be like writing ten or twenty articles (or for fiction, like writing many interconnected short stories)—which it is and isn't.

The first thing I realized that was different about writing a book was that it took much more stamina. I could write a 2,000- or 5,000-word article in a weekend (I could even pull an all-nighter if I had to) and then go on with my life. I never wrote one article right after the other. There was always breathing space.

Writing a book seemed endless, even though I wrote a few pages almost every night. Finishing a chapter just does not give you that same feeling of immediate gratification that you get when you finish an article. And you don't get a check after each chapter either. The deadline seems so far away—until it's right in front of you.

You have to learn to pace yourself for writing a book, and most of the time you learn this on the job. For both this book and my first book, I missed my deadline by about thirty days. This surprised me because I think of myself as a professional writer, and I've never missed a deadline for an article in my entire writing career of twenty-three years.

Six months or a year seems an extremely long time at the beginning of the contract, and it's easy to figure that you'll write a page or two a day and end up with three hundred pages when the deadline comes. Few first-time writers take into consideration the time they'll have to take off for holidays, family vacations, flu, children's illnesses and real difficulties like a death in the family or a divorce, but some of this is bound to come up during the course of a year. And it's hard to make up the lost time.

I now recommend that if you think you can write the book in six months, ask for seven, especially if you've never written a book before. If you deliver early, your editor will usually be overjoyed, although occasionally they, too, are backed up and won't get to the manuscript for a month or two.

If you've based your delivery date on your need for the D&A payment, this could be a problem. Try to make your financial plans flexible enough so that you have enough money for an extra ninety days.

For my first book, which I delivered in May, I had expected the D&A payment to come in by July, which was supposed to pay for the family vacation. However, my editor took two months to read the manuscript and then asked me for additional pages and a reorganization of the chapters (which did make the book better) the week before I left for vacation. I handed in the revised manuscript on September 1, she asked for a handful of additional changes, and I didn't get my D&A payment until December.

Of course, I had this book to write, so every time I had to go back to the first book, I fell further behind on my anticipated writing schedule for the second. Meanwhile, I have a day job that requires a lot of at-home reading, which I was also falling behind on, and I had just agreed to teach a class on being an agent for New York University. All my dreams had come true (two book contracts and an adjunct professorship at my alma mater), and I was in writer hell.

I looked at my life and changed my writing pace. I had been writing a page or two a night—a nice, comfortable pace—but it just wasn't enough. I told my husband and son that I had to write every night, and when I put my son to bed at 9:00 P.M., I wrote until midnight almost every night. I rented no more videos, cut back on my nights out and even stopped reading published fiction (a real luxury for a literary agent, but a necessity, too, or we don't know why certain books make it to the best-seller list). I had been reading *A Man in Full* by Tom Wolfe and stopped, cold turkey, at page 120.

I also remembered the advice that Dean Koontz and Anne Lamott gave in their respective writing books, which I consider to be the basic inspirational tools for any writer. In *How to Write Best-Selling Fiction* (an out-of-print Writer's Digest Book that is a gem—find it at a library and copy it), Koontz says you must put aside a block of time to write, preferably a weekend, with no interruptions. In *Bird by Bird*, Anne Lamott recommends that you promise yourself that you will write at a certain time for a certain amount of time each day and that no matter how you are feeling, you just put words on paper, one word at a time, one sentence at a time, one paragraph at a time, until you have a page.

My method is a compromise between the two—I write each night from 9:00 P.M. to midnight (1:00 A.M. on weekends), but with reasonable interruptions (when you're a working mom, there are always phone calls and sick children), and I never allow myself the luxury of waiting for inspiration. I can always go back and edit, and knowing that makes it a lot easier to just type the words.

GET FEEDBACK

Writing is a lonely profession, and it's sometimes hard to keep telling yourself you're doing a great job when you have no one to show your work to. A spouse, a family member or a best friend will usually read your work if you ask, but their job in your life is to give you support, and a writer needs some professional feedback to keep going, especially if you're rushing to meet a deadline.

This is where your agent, your editor and your writing buddies from your writer's group or organization should come in. If you have a good working relationship with your agent or your editor, ask if they would be willing to read the first chapter to give you some feedback on how the book is going or to tell you if you're on the right track. They usually understand that you just need a little pat on the back and should be willing to read a few pages (ten to thirty) fairly quickly (a week). Don't send them the chapters as you write them, unless they've asked you to.

If a week has gone by (including two full weekends) and you haven't heard anything, it probably means your agent and/ or editor are swamped (and not that they don't love you), and you'll have to go somewhere else for feedback. Even though I know better, when I put on my writer's hat I become as anxious as any author, and I always hope that my editor or agent will be so interested in what I'm doing that they'll drop whatever they have to read and look at *my* work.

Most writers have one really good writing pal whom they can confide in when the writing gets tough. This could be someone you've met on the Internet, through writing classes or through a writer's organization, but it should be someone who understands what it takes to write. Many writers have a reader (not a fan, just someone who has always loved their work and given them good writing advice) whom they actually write for.

If, during the course of writing the book, the direction changes in any important way from that of the outline, you must tell your agent. She will be able to gauge whether this is something you need to present to your editor and also how you should do it. If the book changes during the writing process, it could mean that you are writing a stronger book or that you're going off on a tangent. You don't want to waste time writing a book that your publisher doesn't want and then have to go back and rewrite it according to the original outline.

You should keep in touch with your editor while writing the book. You can do this by sending an E-mail or a simple note telling her briefly how the writing is going, something along the lines of:

> Dear Trish:
>
> I'm about two-thirds through the book now, and I do think I will meet my deadline. I'm really enjoying seeing my characters come alive, and I've kept in mind the suggestions you gave me about keeping the language as active as possible.

Your editor doesn't need to know that a tertiary character has been transformed into a secondary character during the course of the writing or that you decided to split chapter thirteen into two chapters. She can see this when you deliver the manuscript.

When your book is finished, send the completed manuscript to your agent. She probably won't read it, but she will glance at it and will send it on to your editor with a note requesting your delivery-and-acceptance payment. This is the professional way to do things and reminds the editor that you do expect to get paid, so she should read it sooner than later.

THE EDITING PROCESS

You probably won't have much correspondence with your editor until you deliver the book. Unless your editor is fairly new at the house or only does a limited number of books a year, you can expect to wait four to eight weeks for the editorial letter. If this is a first book, you should expect the editorial letter to more or less say "You've done a good job, now here's how I want you to improve it."

If you're not prepared for this, or you've been working so hard on the book that you really think it's perfect, this will come as a real blow. Remember that your editor bought the book because she wanted to work with you, and it's her job to make it better. Say this to yourself a hundred times and resist the urge to dash off a letter explaining why you wrote the book the way you did or how your editor doesn't know the first thing about literature.

Even though editors should know better, they rarely send a copy of the editorial letter to the agent. If you've slept on the editorial letter and you still have a strong reaction to the changes your editor wants you to make, fax the letter to your agent and talk about it.

Your agent will be able to tell you if you have realistic grounds to stand on if you don't want to make the changes. She's sold many books, and can tell whether or not the editor's suggestions will make the book stronger.

Although editors today are rushed for editing time, they do want to make some contribution to the books they buy. Often they really are making good suggestions, which you can improve upon in a way that will make them your own. Few editors are ordering you to do things the way they want them. They just want you to think about your book in a slightly different way.

Occasionally there's a real problem with the vision for the book. After you've calmed down and talked it over with your agent, you might want to call your editor and try to compromise on her suggestions. Most editors will listen, and most will tell you to give the compromise a try. Rarely have I had to pull a book and sell it elsewhere to save an author's vision for his book, but I have had to threaten to do so many times.

In one instance, in a small auction I sold a very dark book by an author who had published two previous novels. When he handed in the book, the editor was aghast at how dark it was and wanted him to change the ending, which he had included in his outline. He was livid, and he was right.

So I called the editor and told her that this was the book she had bought, and if she really didn't like it, I would call the auction underbidder and see if they were still interested. She admitted that she hadn't read the outline because she was so anxious to get the author. She told me she was leaving for another publishing company in a matter of weeks, so she wasn't going to fight over the book. She told me to read the revised manuscript and, if I thought it was OK, to send it on to production. Needless to day, neither the author nor I have done any additional business with her—and the book received excellent reviews.

Most of the time, the author and editor actually grow quite close during the editing process. If you live in the New York area, or are going to a writers conference your editor will be attending, this is a good time for the two of you to meet face to face, which will usually be for lunch. If you haven't met your agent, she may join you as well.

The editor/author lunch is not a social occasion, even though the two of you may now be in love with the book you've just written. Its purpose is to make your editor fall even more deeply in love with you as a writer, so you should shy away from giving her too many personal details that don't enhance you as a writer, while still letting her know all the fascinating things you want to do during your writing career. You should talk a little bit about your next book (but don't give the whole thing away), and your editor should tell you about the publisher's plans for publicity and marketing of the book. If your agent doesn't attend the lunch, call her afterwards and let her know how it went.

Although the author/editor relationship is usually a good one, occasionally it can get too close. One editor who had been working with an author for a number of books offered to lend the author money, which he accepted. When the book was late, the editor called him at home to berate him into finishing the book. The author got so upset with these nightly phone calls that he decided to leave his publisher. It was a very ugly situation all around.

Another author became so enamored of his editor that he listened to no one else about his career. His agent had given him the idea for the book that the editor had bought and walked him through editorial crises so that he wouldn't have to call his editor. His editor didn't like the agent, and repeatedly made disparaging remarks about him, so the author thought he would get more money if he changed agents. After he did so, he received the same advance for his next books and realized that he had now lost someone from whom he could get really good feedback. When he asked around, no one could understand why he had left his first agent (even his new agent), but they did have unkind things to say about his editor. He had the good sense to apologize to his first agent, and they are still on speaking terms.

Once you've revised your manuscript, don't think it's all over. There could be an additional edit before the book is finally accepted, although a really good agent might be able to get the editor to begin processing the D&A payment after the first rewrite.

Once the book has been accepted for publication, you will have to read the copyedited manuscript, and you will have to do this in two weeks. This will include all sorts of queries about your use of language and references, and you will have to check everything before you send it back. A lot of the questions copy editors ask are trite, but that's their job. On my first book, which included fifty pages of recipes, I was asked what size eggs the recipes called for and how much ice was needed for a drink recipe that said "serve over ice."

About four to six months before publication, you will have to read the page proofs, and you will have to do this in two weeks as well. Here you have to catch typesetting errors (sometimes they leave out entire paragraphs). It's your last chance to fix anything before the book goes to press, but you are discouraged from making any big changes, or you will have to pay for resetting the type.

If you're writing nonfiction and you've agreed to do the index, you will receive a second set of page proofs with numbered pages a few weeks after you send back the first set of page proofs. This is a lot of work, and if you're already at work on the next book, your mind will now be somewhere else. Most authors let the publisher do the index and charge the cost of doing it against their royalty account. Your agent may have even negotiated this fee out of the contract or had you and the publisher split the cost.

If you're really lucky, your editor may ask you to type up some jacket copy. This is just to give the jacket copy writers some idea of what you want the jacket to say, but it's also an opportunity to give the book your own spin. Sometimes they even use the author's jacket copy, because it saves them time. The downside of this is that they usually ask you to do it in twenty-four hours, but take the time to do a good job—otherwise someone else will do a worse job for you.

Of course, once you've written and rewritten your first book, there's very little time to bask in the glow of a job well done. Your mind should be filled to the brim with creative panic about what your next book project will be and how fast you can put the sample material together so you can talk to your agent about it.

CHAPTER FOURTEEN

You've Written the Book—Now What?

The Fascinating Worlds of Subrights and Publicity

Once your manuscript is handed in and accepted, it will probably be another three to six months before there is any activity on the book that you can see, which can drive a first-time author crazy. On average, it takes nine months for a book to go from manuscript to publication. About half of that time is used for production of the book (copy editing, cover art, typesetting, indexing, etc.), and the other half is used to get the subrights and publicity machines in gear.

SUBRIGHTS

About five or six months before publication, your agent should receive bound galleys of your book. Some houses try to make the author pay for these out of his royalty account, but if you have a good agent, the cost should be absorbed by the publisher.

These galleys are sent out by both your agent and the publisher's subright's department to places that can buy these rights. The publisher will usually handle the sale to book clubs and after-publication magazine rights (second serial sale), as well as audio and electronic rights if they've been retained by the publisher. Your agent will be sending the galleys to magazines and newspapers for publication in issues that appear on the newsstand at the same time as your book appears in bookstores (first serial), as well as a handful of galleys to her film agent.

Most of the big-circulation magazines ask to see a book five months before publication, so the magazines are the first places to get the galleys. It is possible to sell two different excerpts from the book for first or second serial rights to both magazines and newspapers, but they can't be in the same market. For instance, you *could* sell an excerpt to *Cosmopolitan* and *Maxim*, but you could *not* sell an excerpt to *Cosmopolitan* and *Madamoiselle*. Newspapers and smaller circulation magazines have a shorter deadline, so they usually get the material on the second round of submissions.

Although some books are big enough out of the starting gate to be sent to Europe for sale without quotes and reviews, most agents (or the subrights department) will wait until the first reviews are in (*Publisher's Weekly* and *Kirkus Review* reviews come in about four to six weeks before the publication date) before sending the galleys to their foreign agents. The same goes for film rights. This is usually a month or two before publication.

Foreign agents like to have as much supporting documentation as possible when they send out a book, so they'd rather have the finished book with the quotes and reviews than the galleys. They are rarely willing to send out manuscripts, unless it's a book that has a tremendous "buzz" or it's been requested by an editor and they're fairly certain that they will sell it.

The big foreign rights book convention is held every year in Frankfurt, Germany, in October. Publishers and agents from all over the world descend upon this book fair to tout their wares. Many books are bought at Frankfurt, and many agents and publishers hold off sending things out until then, when they can pitch the books face to face.

Reprint rights used to be a big moneymaker for the author, with paperback rights to commercial fiction going for hundreds of thousands of dollars in huge auctions. This was actually one of the reasons for the publishing merger trend of the late 1980s. The result of these mergers is that today all the major hardcover publishers have their own paperback imprints, so very few books are offered for reprint sale. (See chapter two for an overview of how we got here.)

Most books are bought *hard/soft*, which means that the publisher intends to publish both the hardcover and mass market (or trade paperback) editions. Those that are offered for reprint sale are usually books published by the smaller houses.

The benefit of having your hardcover publisher publish your paperback is that you get full royalties on each edition of the book. When a publisher sells the reprint rights, both the advance and the royalties are split 50/50 between the author and the publisher.

PUBLICITY

Meanwhile, about three months before the book is due to be published you should be assigned an in-house publicist. If this is a first novel, a genre novel or a small nonfiction book, you will most likely be given the most junior person on the publicity totem pole, if you are given anyone at all. She is overworked and underpaid and doesn't have a lot of time for books that can't get bookings on the morning shows.

Let me backtrack a moment and give you my overview of how the publicity departments in major publishing houses work. Publishers print anywhere from fifty to six hundred individual titles a year, but their publicity department is usually staffed by three to six people, one of whom is a glorified secretary (her job is to mail out all those galleys).

Authors such as King, Koontz and Kellerman are the responsibility of the most senior publicist. This person is only interested in the top national media—getting appearances on *Today* and *Oprah*.

Her junior associates are responsible for the local media—the TV and radio shows and interviews with the larger newspapers (*The New York Times*, *The Miami Herald*, *The Chicago Tribune* and *The Washington Post*), as well as author readings at the national book chains (Barnes & Noble, Crown and Tower). There is no one in the department with the time or interest to really go after the college market or specialty presses, such as *The Law Review*. In my experience, most of the time junior associates are too overwhelmed to even send review copies out to local newspapers who have asked for them.

Publicity departments will make you promises with the best of intentions, but the follow-through just isn't there, unless the book surprises everyone and takes off like a rocket. Authors today just have to expect that they will be helping with (if not managing) their own publicity.

However, the author is not helpless. If you received a decent-size advance for the book, it is in your interest to ask your agent to help you find a New York-based or local publicist (especially specialty markets like San Francisco or Miami) whom you can pay about $1,000 (again, this is tax deductible) to aid in getting the word out about your book. Although publicity departments will tell you that this is unnecessary, every one of my authors who did it received much better, and much more, coverage than those who did not.

What the author's publicist can do is really target the book. She doesn't have to worry about the national media, because the publisher is handling that. What she can do is contact the specialty presses who might really be interested in your book (the gay press or the Latino media, for instance), as well as the local and smaller bookstores, whom your publisher just won't have the time to really pressure for an interview, a review or a signing. Of course, she will coordinate this with the publisher's publicity. Since you're paying her, you can expect to get much more feedback than you can from the publicity department.

Of course, the author can do a lot himself. As mentioned previously, editors and agents may be able to send a copy or two of a manuscript out for quotes, but it's really in the author's interest to do this himself. It's best if these requests come with a personal contact, so if you haven't joined a writers organization yet, this is the time to do so. Go to the group's annual convention, and ask your editor or agent to make a call to the event's coordinator to see if you can get on a panel. There's always a "first novel" or "breaking into the field" panel. This will help put you on the map. Meet everyone you can, even if you have to stand in the lobby of the hotel to do so. Go to as many panel discussions as possible, and ask your agent or editor to introduce you to people. Go to the dealer's room and sign every single book of yours they have. You should return home from one of these conventions with at least ten good, solid, new contacts.

If you have a little bit of free time, ask the publicity department to send you the list of people and places to whom they have sent your book for review and interviews. Your agent might have to intervene on your behalf, because the publicity department often guards this list like a crown jewel. One of my authors sat down and wrote a personal note to four hundred magazine and newspaper editors who received his galleys, giving them his home phone number and encouraging them to call him if they wanted any information on how and why he wrote the book. This brought him about ten extra interviews, some of which were in surprisingly large newspapers and some in offbeat presses, that helped place his first novel on *The Chicago Tribune* best-seller list.

You could also do the same for the college newspapers and radio stations, especially those at your alma mater and those in your area. When I was in college working on the university's feature newspaper, we were desperate for original angles on material. While it may not seem like much, you'll at least have a number of clips to send out with your next book, instead of just the reviews, from *PW* and *Kirkus*.

Don't expect your publisher to throw you a publishing party to launch your first novel. You should throw one for yourself, even it's just among friends. If you have a particularly good local bookstore, especially one that features your genre (e.g., a mystery or sci-fi store), call the local store manager and ask if you can hold your publishing party there (offer to supply wine and cheese).

If the local bookstore will host your party, call the local newspaper and get the party listed in the calendar of upcoming events. Perhaps they'll even do an interview with you or cover the event, so make sure you invite the arts editor. If the newspaper doesn't send someone, have someone at the party take a few pictures and send them to the paper. They might run the picture with a caption along the lines of "Local author celebrates publication of his first book at local bookstore." All of this has to be set up two to three months before publication.

REVIEWS

Not all books get reviews. *Publisher's Weekly*, *Kirkus Review* and *The Library Journal* are supposed to review all books that are sent to them, but sometimes the galleys don't get there in time, and sometimes your publisher doesn't print galleys. Reviewers will rarely read unbound manuscripts. Certain kinds of books (genre paperbacks) often are overlooked by reviewers as well because they're just not taken as seriously as hardcover or trade paperback fiction.

Sometimes reviews are bad, and sometimes they're actually mean-spirited, but you can usually find a phrase or a sentence in the most awful review that can be used as a quote on the paperback. One of my horror writers was featured prominently in a scathing review of the "splatterpunk" movement of the late 1980s in *The New York Times*. The review basically called him the best of the worst in contemporary horror, but we used the quote as "best of . . . the splatterpunks."

This is also why quotes from other published writers are so important, because they help supplement the review quotes. You can't control the review quotes, but you do have some say in who you can send your book to for a quote.

Don't allow a bad review to get to you. It's actually the sign that you are now a professional, in the baptism-by-fire tradition.

One of my authors, who had waited twenty years to get published (he grew up with Russell Banks and had studied with Reynolds Price), received almost universally glowing reviews for his first book, but the second review that came in was awful. It was actually the only bad review he got, but he became fixated on it, and it dampened an otherwise stellar debut.

The one thing you can do to help with reviews is to do research in your area of publishing (law, education or romance) and find out which smaller newspapers and magazines publish book reviews. Ask your publicist to call and send them a copy, and if they won't, or don't have the time, do it yourself. You will probably get a review this way.

HOLLYWOOD

Very few books get made into movies, and only a handful more are optioned and then never made into movies. However, the good news is that at this moment in time Hollywood is very interested in making films from books (this is a fluctuating trend). Your book's chances of being optioned depend on the kind of book it is—fiction or nonfiction—as well as the trends in the movie industry, such as whether or not they're looking for science fiction at the moment. What Hollywood was buying last year has almost no bearing on what they want this year.

If your book is optioned, it will mean that a producer has the right to show your book around and look for a studio to lay out money to develop the script. An option is usually for six months or a year, and is a rather small fee (a few thousand dollars) against a larger fee if the studio picks up the option. In the financial pecking order, cable made-for-TV movies pay the least, followed by network made-for-TV movies, with theatrical films paying the most.

It's a long road from option to movie, sometimes taking up to ten years. I've had hundreds of books optioned, but then the option lapses and nothing happens. One book, which was purchased outright (which means the author did get a nice piece of change) by a Disney company in 1992, is now finally far along enough in production that Bruce Willis might actually star in it, but the deal was still not fully in place at the time of this writing.

New York literary agents rarely do their own film deals, because you need to know the story editors and producers who are looking for certain types of books. They're all on the

West Coast, and we're not. Our film agents lunch with them, just like we lunch with the book editors, and a good agent knows what the movie people are looking for before they do. They also know where all the loopholes and pitfalls are in the film contracts (and there are plenty of them).

We use film agents whom we've grown to trust over the years, and split our commission with them, just as we do with our foreign agents. Some literary agents use only one film agent exclusively, hoping that by giving him their loyalty, he will get to their books quickly. I worked in an agency that did this, but the problem was that the agent we had just didn't sell my kind of books. When I left that agency, I went to Hollywood every year to interview film agents and now work with four.

One of my film agents sold a few books for me very successfully, so I tried to pressure him into taking on more of my clients. He kindly explained to me that he thought it was unreasonable for me to expect that he would love my whole list, and that he only took on books he was passionate about (which is my philosophy, too). He likened what I was asking him to do to representing an entire family just because I liked one of the cousins. When he explained it that way, I saw his point.

It is very rare for a novelist to write his own screenplay, although most first-time authors think they can. Screenplay writing is a very specific type of writing, and a studio is not going to lay out money and allow you to learn on the job. Usually they want someone who is *studio-approved*, which means someone who has already received the seal of approval from Hollywood. Sometimes a studio will allow the author to team up with a studio-approved author and learn from him, but this becomes writing by committee, which is very hard for any novelist to take.

The one author I represent who was hired to write his own screenplay found it to be a surprisingly grueling experience. He was paid Writer's Guild minimum (all screenwriters have to join the Guild, which is not a bad thing because they have wonderful health insurance for writers). This deal seemed like an awful lot of money when he signed the contract, but they made him rewrite the script twenty-five times over a year and a half, and he realized he could have written at least three novels during that time.

About halfway through the rewriting process, he called me in tears. The producers wanted him to kill off his favorite character. He wanted to stand on principle, which I explained to him was not a good idea in Hollywood. They would simply hire another screenwriter, who would kill his character off much less gracefully than he would. By the time the script was accepted, it looked very little like the vision he had had in his head and hardly resembled the book at all.

CHAPTER FIFTEEN

THE NEXT BOOK

Outlines, Sample Chapters, Multiple-Book Deals and Waiting

In a perfect world, the author would be offered a contract for another book right after the first book was accepted, and that offer would be a substantial improvement over the last one. But publishing is a far from perfect world.

You should be thinking about your next book as you are editing your first book. You should be having discussions with your agent about what that next book should be. You might even draw up a one-page synopsis and fax or E-mail it to your agent for her feedback. If she's an editorial agent, she can really help you grow the book. This is especially important if you sold your first manuscript as a completed novel, since you probably wrote the first draft completely on your own.

The good news about second books is that you don't have to write the whole thing to get another contract, whether it's fiction or nonfiction. All you need to do is write an outline and as few as one sample chapter; at most you must write the first fifty pages. Your editor should know how you work and how she works with you.

The bad news is that outline writing does not come easily to all writers. Many novelists write organically (which means they let the characters take control of the situation) and aren't really sure how the book is going to go from point A to point B, but they know they'll get there. While this is an admirable and often mystical way to write a first novel, you just can't sell a book that way.

You will need a strong outline to sell your second novel,

because more than one person will be looking at it. Second novels are often notorious flops, because the author spent years writing and polishing the first novel and then raced through the second novel to meet a deadline. How many people remember even the titles of Brett Easton Ellis's or Jay McInerny's second novels? Yet no one can forget *Less Than Zero* and *Bright Lights, Big City*. There's even a phrase for weak second books—the sophomore slump—so you want to be aware of this syndrome before you send something rushed or unpolished to your editor and find yourself without a contract.

Even if your editor loves your book and has big plans for it, she probably won't buy your second book until orders are in for your first book, which could be three to six months after acceptance. This will give the publisher an indication of how the book will sell, but it won't give them an impetus to increase the advance. However, if you really want to get under contract as soon as possible, your editor may be willing to help you develop the next book, which is usually a good thing. This way, she's already invested in it.

The surest way to get a huge increase in the advance for your second novel is to wait until the first book is published to see if you get great reviews and quotes, book club and foreign sales, and maybe even a movie option. Sometimes your editor knows that your book is going to be well received (there was an auction for the book or she is getting a great reaction from the marketing people), so she will try to sign you up at the same advance before you get all the ammunition to ask for a bigger one. This is where your agent becomes very important, because she can play your needs off of those of your editor.

It is slightly easier to sell the next nonfiction book before publication because many of these books fill a slot (celebrity bios, how-to books, humor, etc.), and your publisher knows they'll have another slot open next year. However, you're not likely to get a much bigger advance if your first book's track record is unknown, unless you are some kind of celebrity author and the house just wants to continue to keep you tied up with them.

Oddly enough, the same is true of genre fiction. If your genre is selling well, your publisher will probably be willing to sign you up for the next book without a sales history because they have a slot open for a western or a medical thriller in the coming year. Again, if you do this before the sales figures are in, you won't get much more than what you received for the first book.

This is a hard decision for an author to make, especially since genres do go from boom to bust, sometimes without much warning. As an agent who has lived through one full boom-and-bust cycle of the horror genre (my favorite genre, and the one I know best), my advice to clients who are concerned about money or about making sure that they are publishing a book a year is to get under contract.

MULTIPLE-BOOK DEALS

This is also the thinking behind multiple-book contracts, for both the author and the publisher. Publishers will often offer a two- or three-book deal for genre fiction—especially science fiction, fantasy, romance and men's action adventure—or books in a series. Most of these offers are for the same amount of money per book. A good agent can probably get you slightly more for each book (a deal of $7,000 for the first book, $8,000 for the second and $9,000 for the third).

The pluses to this are that the author knows what he will be writing and how much he will be getting per book two or three years into the future. If he's thinking of buying a house or writing full time, this is an attractive offer.

Also, you don't have to hand in the outlines for the next two books when the deal is made, so there's less work up front. Often the deal will just be for the first novel and two untitled novels in the same genre.

You also get a big signing payment on multiple-book deals. If your agent is good, you can get as much as half the total advance for the three books on signing, and then you get the remaining amount in thirds on delivery and acceptance of each manuscript.

One final benefit to taking a multiple-book contract is that even if the genre you're writing in takes a dive in popularity during the term of your contract, publishers rarely cancel a contract, so you are assured of receiving the money for this deal if you write the books. The worst thing that has happened to some of my authors when the genre collapses is that the publisher pays for the book and decides not to publish it. We are then free to sell it elsewhere and usually can find a home for it, even if it's for less than what the original publisher paid (but you're getting paid twice for one book).

The downside is that these multiple-book offers are usually made as a *joint account* or *basket* deal (see chapter twelve for an explanation of this term), with no flexibility on this point. This is how the publisher can afford to lay out this money. If your books do well, you'll have to wait a long time for the royalties, and you'll be writing books at a price that you know is less than what they're worth.

CHANGING GENRES

Editors never want to hear that an author wants to write in more than one genre, or that a genre novelist thinks he has a literary novel in him. Most of the time you have to change houses, or at least editors, to change genres, but you *don't* have to change agents.

You can change genres or begin a two-track career on your second book, but it may be wiser to get under contract for the same kind of book as your first before you set off on another course.

Most of the authors we represent are, or have been, journalists, or at least professional writers, even if they write fiction. What our literary agency is particularly good at is developing authors who can write both fiction and nonfiction. That is my usual recommendation to my clients who want to write more than one book a year.

One of the reasons I recommend this is that writing fiction

and writing nonfiction take different writing skills, so one book won't drain the creativity of the other. You can spend the morning researching and the afternoon writing fiction, and you won't have two sets of characters fighting with each other when you drift off to sleep.

The bust-and-boom cycles of fiction and nonfiction are very different, too. It's conceivable that you could be writing in two fiction genres that go bust at the same time, but once you have a nonfiction credit under your belt you can always get another contract, even if it's for a different kind of book. If your fiction genre is very competitive, you can write two nonfiction books that year while you polish your novel.

Fiction editors also have the perception that authors shouldn't have too much fiction out in the marketplace at the same time, while they don't think that fiction and nonfiction compete at all. They think it's just great that you've written a horror novel and you're also writing a book on horror films, but if you've written a romance novel and a historical saga in the same year, they may think you're a hack writer.

This perception of being a hack if you write more than one book a year was more likely to be the case in the 1970s and 1980s, when even Stephen King and Dean Koontz had to write under pseudonyms to keep their work published. Now that publishers want more of a good thing, they are more than willing to put as many Stephen King novels out there as possible, even if one bumps the other off of first place on the bestseller list.

If you have to wait for sales figures to sign up your second novel, you can always put your energy into developing a nonfiction book, unless you've decided that you don't want to wait or that you want to change houses or editors.

CHANGING PUBLISHERS OR EDITORS

Sometimes the editing experience is so bad that right from the start an author knows he never wants to do another book with that editor or that publisher as long as he lives. Sometimes the editor who bought the book leaves halfway through the editing or publishing process, and the author wants to follow him. Sometimes the new editor (see *orphaned books* in chapter eighteen) just doesn't get the book or doesn't really consider the author *his* author. Sometimes the publishing company changes its mind about how big a book is and allows it to die on the vine. Sometimes the offer for the second book is even less than for the first one.

These are all good reasons to change publishers or editors, and you should discuss them with your agent as soon as they come up. However, sometimes the author's expectations are unrealistic, and the agent can give him a dose of reality based on what other authors have done in similar situations.

Remember that you have an option with your first publisher, so it's not the simplest thing in the world to change houses—but if you have a good reason, an agent can get you out of your option without totally alienating the first publisher. It has to be worth it, however.

Leaving a publisher for more money is not the best of reasons, unless it's for a lot more money and the first publisher just won't pay what you, the author, are worth. You don't want to get the reputation of being an author who will jump ship at every port, because this is a very small industry and word does get around.

If you've made up your mind that you want to leave, your agent will probably sneak your outline and sample chapters to a few (maybe three) editors who have either expressed interest in your work or are likely to buy the kind of book you're writing. The proposal for either your novel or your nonfiction book must be as polished and as complete as when you sold your first book, which includes a marketing section as well as any quotes or reviews you received.

Your agent will ask these editors to take a quick look at the material to see if they have any interest in stealing the author. They will get back to her within a week. Only when one of the editors has said that he is interested in your work will she begin extricating you from your present option.

One of the easier ways to get out of an option is to send

your partial manuscript in to your editor and start the clock ticking. Your contract will have called for a reaction within thirty or sixty days, and if the editor fails to make an offer in that time, you are free to accept another offer.

Another way to do this is to get a much higher offer from the second publisher, so that when the first publisher comes in with an offer, you can honestly say that the book is worth more. If the first publisher won't meet it, you are free to go to the other publisher.

Sometimes the first publisher surprises everyone and comes up with a higher offer, knowing what your agent is probably doing. If this happens, it is up to the author to decide which house he wants to go with, although morally your first publisher does have the option.

If the dispute was only about money, stay with the first publisher unless the second publisher comes up with a much better offer on this round. Since the second publisher knows that the author had an option at the first house, she will respect that the author decided to stay there even if she's not happy that she lost the book. You also know that you have an interested editor at another house.

If the dispute wasn't about money, but about editing or the way the publisher sold the first book, your agent will have to tell a partial truth to the editor to get you out of the contract. Although it is painful to hear that an author found the publishing process under an editor less than perfect, few editors will want to publish an author who is not happy with them or their publishing house, and they will let the author go. If the dispute was amicable, and the editor thinks the author may one day really go places, they may even leave the door open for the author to come back at a later date.

This is why it is very important to keep these breakups as peaceful as possible. Never tell an editor how you really feel about her work or how the publisher messed up your book, even if it's all true. That editor could become the head of a division where you are published later on in your career. Even if you don't work with her directly, you don't want her to turn down your book or to be less than enthusiastic about allocating marketing resources to your work.

The reason agents sneak work to other editors is that we never want to turn down an offer before we have someplace else to go with the book. We also don't want everyone in the business to know that we're looking for a new house. Although the author may never want to do another book with an editor, sometimes that editor is the only fish in the sea. If that's the case, you might be a little more willing to work with that editor after your agent has tested the market with a sneak submission.

If there has been an irreconcilable difference between you and your editor, your agent may even be able to call the head of the division and see if she can get another editor assigned to the book. However, this is a difficult call to make, because executive editors don't want to hear that an author thinks his editor is not good, and they aren't too thrilled about being told what to do by agents. It's their job to defend their editors; and if they don't at least make the effort, you have to wonder about their management skills and the future of the editor in question. However, if the author has a strong case, the least the executive editor will do is have a talk with the editor. If the editor is also less than enamored with the author, and the agent knows another editor at the house who likes the author's work, an amicable solution can usually be reached.

All of this maneuvering can take a long time, which means that the author may not have another book contract until as long as a year after he's finished his first book. Unfortunately, waiting is a big part of getting published, even when you're a published author.

PART IV

YOUR
CAREER

CHAPTER SIXTEEN

KEEPING IT ALL PROFESSIONAL

Accountants, Lawyers and Writers Organizations

Once you get your first check from writing you are a professional writer, and you should present yourself as one. Editors and agents will now expect you to have the basics of a home office.

This means that if your computer and printer are old and creaky, you should upgrade. You should have a working fax machine, as well as an E-mail account. Your phone should have an answering machine.

You don't need to go out and print up fancy stationery or business cards, but you should have something a bit better than the homemade variety, especially if you are writing to newspaper editors and published authors for reviews and quotes.

You might also want to consider putting up a personal Web site, which many writers do today. This is a good way to get feedback from your fans, as well as to promote your book. Most Internet providers offer a free Web site for personal use in their Internet access fee. If you don't want to learn how to put up the Web site yourself, there will probably be someone in your neighborhood, office or writer's organization who will be willing to teach you, or to do it for you, for a relatively small fee.

If you can't afford a room of your own to write in, you should at least have a private nook of the house or apartment that nobody but you touches. You should have a comfortable chair and a desk, as well as some drawers for filing or a separate filing cabinet. Your files should contain your copies of your contracts, royalty statements, expenses, reviews and writer's organization newsletters, as well as copies of any articles or short stories you've published. You should not commingle your writing files with family files, or you'll never be able to find things when you need them.

The good news about these new expenses is that they are all tax deductible, and you are now entitled to deduct them. Unbeknownst to most writers, your entire way of bookkeeping changes when you become a published writer, because almost anything you do or buy that is writing related is now tax deductible, including the cost of the accountant himself!

YOUR ACCOUNTANT

You need an accountant now, and not some friend of a relative who does bookkeeping on the side. The reason you need a real accountant is that you are now going to file an itemized tax return instead of the quicker 1040, and it's almost impossible to do this properly yourself because you will miss deductions that you are entitled to. If you used an accountant in the past, expect that he will charge you more for this expanded tax return because it takes him more time to prepare your tax form, but the benefits far outweigh the initial upfront cost.

The first thing you need to do is to make sure your accountant knows how to file a return for your writing business. Most of the authors I represent do not use a generic accounting service such as H&R Block for this. Instead, they ask other writers in their locality for recommendations of accountants who have done a good job for them. This is another reason to join a writers organization, so you can tap your writer friends for a recommendation that you can trust. This is *not* the sort of recommendation you should expect to get from your agent or your editor, because they usually don't know the ins and outs of the business side of being a writer.

Once you've found an accountant you can trust, and who understands how to prepare a tax return for a writer, you need to reorganize how you keep your records. You will be able to take a whole new world of deductions—and you should. These include:

- Phone calls to your agent and editor, and even your writing pals
- Internet access fees
- Books, magazines and newspaper subscriptions
- Memberships in writers organizations
- Writing classes and classes related to your book subject (even the cost of an advanced writing degree)
- Travel-related writing expenses
- Transportation when in New York visiting your editor and agent
- An independent publicist's cost
- Mailing costs
- Paper, ink and copying costs
- Software
- Even your writing desk, chair or computer and printer, if you bought new equipment once you received your first check

The extra added bonus to this second career is that you can also deduct the cost of one room of your home if you use it exclusively as a study or den to write in. That's a lot of deductions.

There are a lot of things you *can't* legitimately deduct, such as new clothes for your meeting with you editor, a leather carrying case for your work in progress or a silk smoking jacket that you wear when writing. You might be able to deduct the cost of babysitting while you're on a business trip or meeting with your editor, but you can't deduct child care without a good reason. Discuss the more creative deductions with your accountant and see what he says. He should be your touchstone of what is permissible.

You have to keep accurate records, and you have to keep receipts. There are many ways to do this, but some of the easier ones are to set up a separate phone line for business calls, faxes and Internet access (this way you can just add up the phone bill checks you write) and to open a credit card that you use exclusively for business-related purchases and expenses, such as travel and meals. Interest carried from month to month on a credit card is not deductible, so I recommend that you open an American Express card for this usage. However, the annual membership cost *is* deductible.

I keep my out-of-pocket receipts in an empty coffee can. These include taxi receipts and incidental supplies, such as batteries or one bottle of whiteout. For big supply orders, I order from Quill or Staples and put it on my writing credit card. Wholesale clubs such as Costco and Sam's also have good prices on supplies, but I use Quill and Staples because they deliver, and delivery is free for larger orders.

Once you begin submitting an itemized tax return, there's a good chance that during the course of ten years you will be audited once. This is not because the IRS doesn't believe you; it's because there aren't that many people doing what you're doing. The IRS just wants to make sure that your deductions are accurate and that you're telling the truth (they may want to see the room you write in).

I've been audited by the IRS once, and when I showed up with my neat little checks and receipts and my organized American Express bill, the audit was painless. I did try to take the cost of dry cleaning my clothes and a leather briefcase off as tax writeoffs, so I had to pay the back taxes on those deductions, which came to something like $100, but they had asked me to verify more than $10,000 in deductions, which I was able to do.

Your agent will send you a 1099 tax form at the end of January, which will tell you how much you made from writing in the previous calendar year. You must attach this to the tax form you file in April, just as you would a W2 form from your employer.

Your agent must report what she paid you to the IRS, so there is no way that the government is not going to know about your writing income. Don't even think about asking your agent to lie to the IRS for you. Your publisher sends your agent a 1099 for the money she receives from the publisher on your behalf, so there is a consistent system of recording where the money has been sent.

YOUR LAWYER

Sometimes writers decide to set up a separate business for this writing career and either incorporate or file a DBA (Doing Business As) certificate. The reasons for this can be as simple as wanting to have a clear separation of family income from writing income to the more complicated issues of protecting yourself from lawsuits (especially if you write celebrity bios or unauthorized pop-culture books about licensed products). Whatever the reason, if you are going to set up a separate company, you should do this with a lawyer.

If you are going to go to the trouble of setting up a separate writing business, you should find a lawyer who understands publishing. You should be able to do this from your writer contacts, or by calling the lawyers who advertise in *Publisher's Weekly*. They won't be much more expensive than the guy down the street, and once you become a client, you will have someone you can call on should you ever really need a lawyer.

WRITERS ORGANIZATIONS

Throughout this whole book I have advocated that writers join professional writers organizations, and I can't stress this enough. However, it's especially important for the beginning writer.

Writers organizations give you so much for your membership dollar that I can't think of a good reason why you should refrain from joining, even if you've never joined a single organization in your entire life. Writing is a lonely profession, and these writers organizations are the one place where you will feel like you belong.

I've never been much of a joiner, because the things I like to do are fairly solitary (reading, writing, painting, etc.). I dropped out of the Girl Scouts as soon as my mother would let me, and I never played team sports. So when I attended my first convention of the Horror Writers of America, I was filled with trepidation, even though I was going as an agent, which I knew gave me an excuse for being there.

Some of the editors I had sent manuscripts to introduced me around, which I will always be grateful for, and before I knew it I was deep in conversation with other people who had grown up reading the same books I had. It was such a joy (and a freedom) to be talking about the literary worth of Stephen King and Anne Rice, whose work I really knew, instead of trying to keep up with a conversation about John Updike or Norman Mailer. By the time the convention was over, I had met a whole bunch of people who could really help my career, and who I really liked, such as established authors who could give quotes to my authors and writers who wanted me to represent them. I also got to know the editors I was sending work to much better.

Looking back on those early writers conventions I attended, I can see that I met some of my favorite and longest-lasting clients there. We were all starting out at the same time, and we clicked really well. I don't know if we would have found each other had we not been at the same place at the same time.

Writers organizations give you contacts and information, as well as friends in the same situation. The newsletters are valuable for news about what's selling and where markets are opening up, especially in smaller arenas like short story anthologies and magazines that publish short stories, which your agent might not know about or might not even want to represent you for. The organization's archives can give you an overview of your genre, the issues it has faced over the years and the gossip that you will not be able to get from a book. The panels at the conventions run the gamut from how to write to how to sell yourself.

Belonging to a writers organization also gives the writer a bit of clout, which is important at the beginning because you feel like you've entered into a maze where you don't know the rules. When you say that you are a member of a professional writers organization, editors and agents know that you consider yourself a professional. They also know that if you are having a serious problem with something, you can ask the organization for advice, and you will get it.

In addition, there are the annual awards given out by the organization, which you should not necessarily expect to win, but which you may get nominated for if the members know who you are. This is always good for a new writer's career.

Writers organizations also offer professional services, such as references for lawyers, accountants, publicists and Web designers, as well as health insurance and even loans for writers who are truly having hard times. Where else could $50 to $100 get such a return on its investment?

There are a few downsides to writers organizations, but they're actually the same for any kind of organization, and that is that members occasionally get into war with each other and ask the membership to choose sides. The best thing to do is just to ignore the fracas and concentrate on your career. If you've become a target of someone, ignore the tirade. If you don't respond, the shooting will stop.

Don't bother your editor or agent with these internal squabbles, no matter how hurtful they are. Unless someone is making libelous charges against you (that you plagiarized your book), it really is just a pissing contest. Involving outsiders will only make you look unprofessional.

The more seriously you take the professional aspects of your career, the more professional you will appear to those whose opinions you value—your editor, your agent, your writing peers and even your readers. Before you know it, you will be the established writer newcomers come to for advice.

CHAPTER SEVENTEEN

MANAGING YOUR WRITING CAREER

Deciding When (and Whether) to Quit Your Day Job

Everyone who has ever enjoyed the experience of writing dreams about doing it full time. The fantasy of doing what you love and getting paid for it is alluring. So is the appeal of not having to get up in the morning and commute to a job where there's someone telling you what to do and how to do it.

But writing is not a get-rich-quick scheme, and books don't write themselves. Every author I know who makes his living from writing puts in as many hours, if not more, than the guy next door who works a day job. It's just that his hours are different, so it looks like he's not working as hard.

Of the fifty writers I represent, only ten make their living exclusively from writing, and they all have multiple-book contracts, which means they write a minimum of two books a year. That's not because they don't make enough per book, it's because the money comes in only once or twice a year, and sometimes there are delays. You can't tell American Express or the bank that holds your mortgage that your editor made you do an extensive rewrite so it will be another thirty or ninety days until you send out the check.

Another ten of my authors have part-time or side-income jobs to supplement their writing careers. What this means is that they really have two jobs.

Let's talk turkey about writing income. If you live in a big city or in a surrounding suburban area, you will need to make between $40,000 and $50,000 a year from your writing. If you live in the country, you might need a little less, say $25,000 to

$35,000. Unless your parents left you the house you're living in or you've moved back in with them, that means that you have to pay monthly bills of $2,000 to $5,000. A $25,000 signing payment goes awfully fast at this rate, and if you miss your deadline, you're in trouble.

The average book receives an advance of $5,000 to $15,000. A worst-case scenario is that you have to write ten books a year to make ends meet. Even if one of your books goes for $25,000, that's still a lot of writing.

Of course, as an author moves forward in his writing career, he can usually expect a slight increase in his advances (but it's not like working for a company where you get an annual raise). If he's lucky and he's writing the right kind of books, the author might see some subsidiary income in the form of foreign and first serial sales, but these usually aren't too big— $2,000 for a magazine excerpt and $2,000 to $5,000 for a foreign sale. Your book may get optioned by Hollywood, but the option will usually be $2,500 to $5,000 as well. And you can't bank on any of it until there's a deal. Even if you sold French rights to your previous novel, there's no guarantee that they'll pick up the next one, even if it's the second in a series.

There are additional expenses that come with having your own business, which is what you are doing when you become a full-time writer. Most small businesses fail because the owners didn't budget properly, or spent too much in setting up the business and couldn't make it back fast enough.

So, make a budget and try to stick to it, and don't overspend in getting set up. If you need to buy new equipment, you don't have to have the latest or the most advanced, as long as it does a good job. You can also lease some of your equipment or pay it off in installments.

If you have to buy office furniture, you don't have to buy the desk of your dreams, because nobody is going to see you working. You can buy that exact replica of Raymond Chandler's desk when one of your books makes extra money. Meanwhile, you can buy something cheaper and put it on your credit card, so you can pay it off over time.

You can also buy used office furniture. In Manhattan (and I'm sure the same is true for most cities) there are office furniture liquidators that buy desks from banks and insurance companies that are expanding or merging; their furniture looks like new, and at a fraction of the cost. I furnished my whole downtown office in used office furniture, with each room in the office having its own style (my office has an antique mahogany desk and bookcase from my family, as well as a fireplace mantle; my partner went with the Sam Spade look). Visiting editors always comment that our office has a real warmth and character that they don't see in their publishing companies because every cubicle looks alike until you get to the corner offices.

When you run your own business, you now have to pay your own health insurance, which can run $300 a month for an individual in this managed care universe we're now living in. Don't even think about going without insurance. If something happens to you, no one else will write your book, and it will take you years to climb out of the health care debt.

One of my authors decided to quit his day job when I got him a two-book deal. He swore to me that he knew what he was doing, and that he had allocated every dime he was going to spend until he delivered the first book. He was single and very frugal, so I hoped that he was right. About two months before his book was due, he called me in tears. He had no money left for food, because he had broken his leg and the cost of the emergency room visit had completely used up the remainder of his advance. He had sold his desk and was writing on the floor. I managed to get him a partial D&A payment from the publisher, but he literally went without food for three days until the check arrived.

You will also have to pay quarterly taxes—your agent or your publisher will not be withholding taxes from your payments. Even with all the deductions you're now entitled to, it will feel like you're paying more in taxes, because it's hard to send the IRS four checks of at least $1,000 if you only get paid once or twice a year.

I'm told that you can take your book contract to a bank and borrow against it, but I don't know any writer who has done this successfully. You may have to borrow from friends and relatives between payments, and this can be hard on your self-esteem, especially if they're the kind of people who like to remind you of the debt, even after you've paid it. It's also hard to think of yourself as a successful writer when you owe your father-in-law the down payment for the house.

Don't expect to borrow money from your agent. She represents many writers and can't be lending one writer money without offering the same service to others, and she can't afford to lend money to fifty clients.

Don't expect your editor to give you more money before you hand in the book. This went out with the family-owned book publishing company. Your agent can ask if the circumstances are dire enough (the author should never discuss money with the editor), but the editor can say no, and there's nothing you can do about it. Whining does not help.

When most of my writers get into financial trouble, what they end up doing is charging up their credit cards and taking cash advances that they will be paying off for years to come. This is not the best approach to financial planning, but if you are thinking about quitting your day job, I would suggest that you apply for as many credit cards as possible while you are employed by someone else, so that you can have them as insurance if the going gets tough. It will be harder to get credit cards once you're self-employed. Having these multiple lines of credit that you use only during emergencies may mean the difference between meeting your deadline and eviction.

If you have a supportive spouse or family, it may be easier to become a full-time writer. Many writers make a deal with their spouse or family that they will be self-supporting in a year or two, and the family saves up enough to limp through the lean times. Before you quit your job, you should have three month's expenses in the bank, on top of the advance payment.

If your spouse works full time, he or she can pick up the cost of health insurance through the job, which is always cheaper than getting it on your own. With all the deductions you're now entitled to, your spouse's withholding taxes may be large enough to cover what you have to pay, but the days of tax refunds are a thing of the past. Your spouse's paycheck will also make it easier to pay the monthly bills, and there may even be a bit of slack for late payments from publishers.

HOW AND WHEN TO GO FULL TIME

Unless you've received a large advance for your first book (over $50,000), you should not quit your day job after you sell it. You need to have the full experience of writing a book, which includes the editing and rewriting process, so you can really know what getting a book published feels like for you in terms of the workload. Once you've done that, you will have a much better idea of how long it really takes you to write and research a 300-page manuscript.

Once you have an offer for your second book, if it is also for a substantial amount of money, you can consider leaving your day job. There's the possibility of subsidiary rights sales on your first book, and there's the delivery payment for the second. Even if your first book deal is for two or three titles, don't quit your job until you've finished the first book.

However, I would recommend that you try working part time first, if your employer will let you. Take one or two days a week to write (Mondays and Fridays will give you a four-day weekend) and see if you like writing during the day, every day. Some writers just aren't as creative from 9:00 A.M. to 5:00 P.M., so there's no reason to quit the day job if they don't write well during the day. Some writers can't write for eight hours at a time.

Some companies will give you a leave of absence, especially if you are writing a book that is related to your field (most newspapers have this kind of agreement). What a leave of absence or working part time can give you is continued health insurance, pension and tenure, as well as the knowledge that your job will still be there if you change your mind or don't meet your expectations.

If you've written and published a number of books, even if none of them has received a large advance, and you know how long it takes you to write a book, you can also consider going full time as a writer. The big "if" here is that you are going to have to increase the number of books you write per year to support yourself, and you have to be fairly certain that the contracts are there.

Once you make this decision, you should have a long talk with your agent. You need to tell her how much you want to make, and how much you absolutely *need* to make, a year. You have to decide just what kind of writing you would be willing to do to pay the bills, because a lot of the work your agent will bring you will not be the kind that gets you nominated for awards.

WORK-FOR-HIRE

You must also be aware that there is no such thing as quick money from writing. The quickest money is in TV tie-in or movie novelizations (all those Star Trek, Batman and Godzilla books out there) because they need to be written in three to six weeks, but you won't get paid for six to eight weeks, because all money still has to go through the contracts and accounting departments.

Agents hate novelizations and tie-ins because they are *work-for-hire*, a term that means that the author does not share in additional revenue from the book's sale. If you're really lucky, you may get a 1 or 2 percent royalty on sales in the United States and Canada, but you won't get any money from the sale of editions to foreign countries. So these kinds of books are one-shots—you get what you're paid upfront and rarely see another dime.

Tie-ins and novelizations usually involve a studio or licensee, which must approve everything, and they often hold up the processing of the payments because they don't really care about when the author gets paid. One of my authors wrote three young adult Star Wars books, and the underlying contract between the publisher and the studio wasn't signed until the third book was published.

You can't be too creative with the characters or storylines of these kinds of books, because there's a preexisting universe that you have to fit your work into. There's either a shooting script or a storyline bible that you must follow.

The studios and licensees also make the author jump through hoops to get these writing assignments, which usually pay $5,000 to $12,000. They want to see your published work, an outline and even a chapter or two on speculation. It's nearly impossible to get one of these books for someone who has not published in the genre of the film or television show, so you can't write a Star Trek novel if you haven't published a science fiction novel. And there are hundreds of writers willing to do this kind of work.

Yes, this kind of work will get your name out there, and yes, it helps the author pay the bills, but it's never as easy as it seems. One of my authors very badly wanted to write a young adult horror novel in a popular series. He did the requisite outline and chapters, and we waited eleven months until he was given the green light. By the time the offer came through, we had signed him up for so many other projects that he could hardly fit it into his schedule.

There are other kinds of writing-for-hire as well. If a publisher develops a series, such as Sweet Valley High or Animorphs, they will create an author name and then have a number of authors write the actual books, which means that your name doesn't go on the cover. These kind of arrangements pay a slightly higher royalty to the author (as high as 4 percent) and sometimes even offer a portion of the foreign rights money. You still have someone else's bible to follow, however, and it's still not your own work.

As I mentioned in chapter fifteen, what our agency recommends for authors who want to make a living as writers is that they have a two-track career, where they write both fiction and nonfiction. There are a number of publishers who know that we represent working writers who can write on demand,

and they come to us on a fairly regular basis with a list of books they are looking for. We prenegotiate the deal so we can tell the author how much the book will bring in, and then if he is interested in writing the book, he does a brief outline. We fax it to the editor, and if he likes it the deal is done. This is easiest to do with nonfiction, but we have been able to develop novels this way as well. It's rare that books like these have a shot at the best-seller list.

If an author writes nonfiction, his agent might be able to get him a celebrity bio or a ghostwriting gig. (The author can go after these himself, too.) The celebrity or expert usually gets two-thirds of the advance and royalty moneys. However, if the author has a certain expertise or reputation himself, the celebrity may be willing to split 50/50. Sometimes one agent represents the writer and another the celebrity.

Before a single word of the book proposal is written, your agent will draw up a collaboration agreement between you and the celebrity. This will lay out the terms of the deal and the obligations of each party, as well as any additional clauses that might be special to this deal. (See Appendix C for a sample collaboration agreement.)

Once the collaboration agreement is signed, the writer will draw up a full proposal for the book, including at least one sample chapter. Sometimes you get a fee for writing the proposal; sometimes you negotiate a higher split. Then your agent or the other agent will send the work out and see if someone bites.

Occasionally celebrities want to write fiction (a *Star Trek* actor, for instance). They may collaborate with a published novelist to develop the book, and they may even give the writer a credit of some kind.

Some genre novelists write both adult and young adult fiction in their genre or a related genre. If you have kids, and you remember what you were reading when you were twelve, this is something to consider. The downside is that there are real limits to language, subject matter and situations in the young adult market, and you have to get to know what's selling there before you present yourself to those editors.

Some authors are embarrassed by the work-for-hire or young adult work they're doing to pay the bills. Some are concerned that their writing peers or editors might think they are hacks if they have too much out there in the marketplace with their name on it. Some writers have two completely different careers in two completely different genres (science fiction and mystery) and are afraid they will be typecast. This is when an author develops a pseudonym.

I don't like pseudonyms, and none of my authors are publishing under pseudonyms at the moment. I'm proud of all the deals I've made for my authors, and I think they should be proud of the fact that they can meet multiple deadlines and write in someone else's universe, but I know others disagree.

One of my authors writes in multiple genres, both adult and young adult fiction as well as nonfiction. Everyone he knew said he should develop a pseudonym, but I told him that all his works complemented each other (it is all in science fiction, fantasy or horror) and that readers in the field would quickly get to know who he was. Within three years, I had editors begging me for his work, because they know he is a professional writer and always delivers polished prose on time. They don't care that he writes at least six books a year. He's been a full-time writer for six years and makes more than any of his peers who started writing at the same time as he did.

THE PRACTICALITIES OF WRITING FROM HOME
Working from home is a difficult thing to do, especially if you are trying to be creative. There are more interruptions than you can imagine, and no one, from the mailman to the Federal Express guy to your mother-in-law (especially your mother-in-law) thinks you're *really* working. They think you're selling drugs, eating bon bons or are independently wealthy. If your spouse is out working, they think you're a golddigger or a gigolo. It wasn't until I forced books into the hands of every single one of the people I came in contact with through the

course of doing business that they really understood that I was running a business myself.

If there are children in the home, the at-home spouse usually takes on the child care job to save some money, ferrying children back and forth to school and playdates. In my experience, the at-home person somehow becomes the person more responsible for the cleanliness of the home and the dinnertime meals. Although this can be a bonus for someone who hasn't had a lot of time with his children, it can also be quite a shock to go from uninterrupted work blocks of at least eight hours to catching four or five hours of time between household chores and child care duties.

I worked from home for five years (not as a writer, but as an agent), and there are a few interesting side effects of this situation. Most of the other people who are home during the day are the mothers of young children who don't work or who work part time. These are the people you will see day in and day out at the supermarket or the local Starbucks. They will want to socialize, but you can't because you have to work. Most of them don't understand this.

It's lonely working at home, too. Your work friends are all busy during the week, so the social life of an office disappears. If you go to lunch with old friends, you are usually the one doing the traveling, because they're working, so you lose a lot of your writing time on a lunch day.

If you're enjoying working from home (and you should, because this is your life's dream), your spouse and former co-workers might resent your new life. They hate their jobs, and you don't. Everyone you meet is inspired by your success, and they want to work from home too. They want the name of your agent and your editor, and they want to collaborate on a book with you. They think it's easy.

If you've made a deal with your spouse, you might find that he now wants to work from home too. If your spouse has a frustrated creative side, he may now say that he wants to try working full time at that avocation.

It's never as easy or as simple as it looks.

CHAPTER EIGHTEEN

WHEN DISASTER STRIKES

Orphaned Books, Cancelled Books, Options Declined, Mergers and Closings

Publishing is a complicated business, and right now it's a business in transition. There are so many shifting trends in the industry at this time that the only thing a writer can be sure of is that nothing will be the same as it was the year before, and certainly not the decade before.

Because of all these changes, things that once happened rarely in publishing are becoming more and more common. Many of these changes are bad for the writer, and therefore they're not so terrific for his agent, but writers and agents must learn to change with the times.

When I started in this industry fifteen years ago, it was very rare for one of my authors' editors to leave during the year and a half it took to write and publish a book. It was expected that editors would stay at their jobs two to three years, and they were often promoted from within their own companies. That's not the case today. Editors change houses sooner and more frequently than snakes shed their skins.

Although a writer should like working with his editor, it's almost dangerous to think that she will *always* be there for him. She'll be there for him (perhaps to even buy his next book), but she might be at another house when the book is published. As soon as an editor buys a book, I now tell my authors that there's a good possibility that his editor will leave before the book is published. I would say that of the one hundred or so books I sell a year, about thirty of them are published under different editors than those that acquired it.

ORPHANED BOOKS

A book becomes *orphaned* when your editor leaves the company and you are saddled with a new editor. Many writers feel devastated by the loss of their editor, especially if they've worked closely with her on developing the book or if they have a multiple-book contract. They are worried that the new editor won't care about the book or about their career, and they are concerned that their in-house champion is now gone.

Although it would be wonderful if I could say that these are unjustifiable fears, they are often the case when a book is orphaned. As soon as your editor leaves (she usually calls your agent first, and then calls her authors herself her last week on the job), you should find out who your new editor is. Your agent will be working on this, too. Sometimes your agent knows the other editors at the house well enough to recommend that your book be assigned to someone who she thinks will like it, if not love it, but the final decision is up to the publisher, who often doesn't like taking suggestions from agents.

Once you've been assigned a new editor, unless you know you can't work with her ("Oh, no. Not her. I called her an 'ignorant pig' at Bouchercon."), you should call and introduce yourself over the phone. Tell her a little bit about what you're writing and ask her in what way she'd like to work with you. Each editor has her own style (E-mail versus fax versus phone). You have to assume that your editor told her next to nothing about you and your book, and you will have to educate her. If you're going to be in New York, or you're going to a convention and she is attending, go out of your way to meet your new editor.

Your agent will be doing the same thing. If she already knows the editor, she can give you her take on the new editor. If it's a new editor who she doesn't know, or an editorial assistant who's just been promoted to take on these orphaned books, your agent will quickly make a lunch date with her. She will then give you her assessment of this new editor (young and eager, conservative, inexperienced, etc.), but she won't be able to judge how well you'll work together.

If you and your new editor don't click, you'll have to take a more active role in promoting your book in-house. Write your own jacket copy, send your new editor all relevant clips and quotes and keep on top of all the deadlines for subrights-related sales. (When will you send galleys? Who's my publicist? What's my print run?) Your agent will be doing this too, but she has fifty other authors' careers to manage, so you have to keep on top of the situation.

The worst case of orphaning we've ever experienced was one where the writer ended up having four editors over the course of two years. Editor #1 loved the book and saw really big things for it. Unfortunately, he left right before the manuscript was handed in. My business partner spoke to the publisher, requesting a like-minded editor, but they had just hired someone who was supposed to do these kinds of books, so they gave it to him. Unbenownst to his publisher, Editor #2 had a reputation among agents as being extremely lazy, so we were all less than pleased when he was assigned the book, but we hoped his work habits had changed.

That was not the case. He sat on the manuscript for four months and, without reading it through, said it would have to be completely rewritten, and that he wasn't even sure that it was publishable. The author was in a panic. We were livid, and we started sending the manuscript around to see if someone else would pick it up without changes. In the midst of this, we received a phone call from the publisher informing us that Editor #2 had been fired, and the assistant to Editor #1 who had bought the book had been promoted and assigned to the book.

We were elated, because he already knew about the book. Editor #3 read it in one weekend and said it hardly needed any editing. We were filled with joy and enthusiasm, and the author quickly went about getting quotes from William Styron and Arthur Miller.

Then Editor #3 called to inform us that he too was leaving. The book had now been assigned to the editor we had asked for after the Editor #1 left, which we thought was good news. The book was already scheduled and edited, so it seemed as though things should work out fine.

Editor #4 had also recently been promoted, and he was now in charge of developing a whole new line of books, which this book did not fit into. He saw himself in a purely caretaking role. The author had been invited to be part of a press conference featuring Miller and Styron in New York, and when she asked if the publisher would like to be involved, Editor #4 was less than enthusiastic about setting things up.

This was truly a nightmarish publishing experience, although the book did get a film option and received a lot of attention and great reviews. Imagine what could have happened if someone at the publishing company had cared?

CANCELLED BOOKS

Even with all the changes going on in the publishing industry today, publishers rarely cancel book contracts. It's just bad for business. Word will get out, and agents and authors will be wary about doing business with them.

With that said, contracts are cancelled occasionally, usually because the author is extremely late with the manuscript. However, sometimes publishers use a tardy delivery as an excuse to cancel a book that they feel they overpaid for, or that they feel the market has changed on. So the best insurance against cancellation is on-time delivery.

If you've missed your deadline, and your book has been cancelled, there's not much you can do at that house. You and your agent will have to try to sell the book elsewhere. Your contract should have a *first proceeds* clause, which states that the author has one year to resell the book and that the first proceeds from that sale (the signing payment) will be sent to the first publisher to pay back the money that has been advanced. If the book is good, and you're a professional writer, you and your agent should be able to find another home for it within that year, but it's extra work for the agent. Agents do not return the commission they took on the first sale. If there's enough money on the second sale, the author might elect to pay it back. Otherwise the publisher usually eats the agent's commission.

Sometimes you can't sell the book for what the first publisher paid for it because the market has crashed or they really did overpay for it. In that case, you pay as much of the advance back as you can, and the publisher eats the loss.

Very rarely you can't find a second publisher. If your agent can show that you really tried to resell the book (and who wouldn't?), most publishers will just write off the advance paid as a loss. They rarely come after the author.

However, if a lot of money was advanced, it's not as easy to shrug your shoulders and say you couldn't resell the book. Sometimes they send a law firm after the author to try to collect the advance.

One time I represented an author who had a big book, missed his deadline by two years and had his contract cancelled. It was the author's fault; he just hadn't been writing the book like he was supposed to be doing, but he *had* spent the money. Everyone in the industry knew that he had missed his deadline, so no one wanted to sign up the book again. When the collection law firm came knocking, he had nothing to give them, so he filed for bankruptcy. It was an extremely sad case, because his writing career was over, too. And the saddest thing was that it could have all been avoided, if he had only taken his deadline more seriously.

I have had other books cancelled for other reasons. One was requested by an editor who left the company and, after it had been accepted and paid for, a whole new editorial regime was in place. They didn't like the concept of the book and refused to publish it. We couldn't resell it either, but they let the advance go.

I once had a whole *line* of books cancelled, but that, too, was the author's fault. I sold three graphic novels to a publishing company for a sizable amount of money. They had just embarked on a new graphic novel line, but when the first books in the line were published, they had real problems with the authors, and the sales were not as good as they had hoped. Meanwhile, my author had a three-book contract sitting unsigned on his desk for six months. He had a lot of other deals that he was doing that were much bigger than this one, and when he hadn't signed the contract in six months, the publishing company just decided to drop the graphic novel line completely.

I will tell you one more cancelled-book horror story before I go on to the nightmare of dropped options. This did not happen to one of my authors, but I know the author it happened to, so it is an unfortunately true story that should make your blood run cold.

There once was a genre novelist who had been toiling in the fields of his trade for many books. When his genre grew in popularity, one of his novels sold hundreds of thousands of copies.

His agent moved him to another publisher, who gave him a stunningly large two-book deal. He wrote a good novel and they gave it a good cover, but the book did not do half as well as its predecessor.

His new publisher had just bought another publisher, and the MBAs were now looking over the company's books. They decided that the second book in the contract was not going to earn nearly enough to justify this large contract, so they cancelled the second book.

I don't know if he got to keep the signing payment, but I do know that he was stunned and devastated, especially since he had bought a large house based on this new stream of revenue. Of course, everyone in publishing knew that he had received this large advance from the new publisher, and that the first book had been disappointing, so no one would pick him up at the price he was now asking. He had to go back to his first publisher for less than he had gotten for the book that had sold hundreds of thousands of copies.

OPTIONS DECLINED

Publishers have a clause in the contract that gives them a legal and moral first look at your next book, which is called the *option*. To have your option declined is a truly frightening thing for an author, especially if you've written a number of books for one publisher, such as a mystery series. It's one thing to leave your publisher because you think you can do better elsewhere; it's quite a different thing to be told you're not wanted anymore.

Sometimes a declined option can be a good thing. Sometimes your publisher really doesn't know how valuable you are, and when you dress yourself up and take your wares elsewhere, you realize it was all for the best. Sometimes it makes you reevaluate your career, and you change directions slightly and head off on a new, and more successful, course.

If you're lucky, one of the editors you've had during the course of your writing career has now moved to another house and is eager to acquire you again. Sometimes an editor will even help you polish your outline for the new house.

Even if you've published ten books, it's always scary to hear that you have to find a new publisher, especially if you are making your living from writing. You and your agent will now strategize, and she will test the marketplace with your new work. Most of the time there will be another publisher who is anxious to pick you up, usually for more money than the first.

Occasionally your publisher is right, and the book you are trying to sell is just not marketable. You'll have to come up with another proposal or an outline for a novel and go out there again. You just keep doing this until something clicks, or until some editor comes up with an idea for your books.

One of the authors I represent has had to change publishers three times in her writing career: Each time she's dreaded it, and each time it's been better for her career. Her first book was sold to a house that did an OK job with it, but her editor left, and no one was really watching the book's progress.

Her next book had a celebrity attached to it, and she was told that she had to try the celebrity's publishing house first. They made her an offer so low that we had to turn it down, but I knew there was another editor at one of that house's imprints who wanted to do the book, so we sent the proposal there and they bought it. Of course the editor left and we were assigned a new editor, but the relationship worked well enough that my author wrote four more books for them in collaboration with the celebrity.

However, one day there were no more books that my author could write with that celebrity, and she was approached by another celebrity to write his book. Her publisher made it clear that they would not publish this book and that they declined the option. The editor who had bought her first book was now at another house, so we sold the new celebrity book to him.

After two books with the new publisher, her option has been declined again, because her editor has been promoted to another division of the company that doesn't publish the kind of books she writes. But this time around, my author has such a stellar reputation and publishing track record that I actually have a list of editors who have approached me about publishing her. Of course she's nervous about her future, but I'm certain she'll find a new home where she's genuinely appreciated.

MERGERS AND CLOSINGS

When one publisher buys another, there's a brief period of elation, especially if the company that's been bought was having a hard time. Editors tell agents and writers that the parent company has assured them that everything will be exactly as it was; meanwhile they're distracted because they're running their resumes off on the company photocopier and meeting with headhunters. Six months to a year after the merger, the blood of sacked editors runs red through the streets of New York.

Sometimes the books acquired by the fired editors are reshuffled to the remaining editors. Sometimes whole lines of books are cancelled or discontinued. The publisher's PR people will present this mass book cancellation as a one-time getting-their-house-in-order bloodletting. If this happens, you can probably keep whatever advance you've been paid, but you'll have to resell the book and find another publisher.

Although mergers are truly frightening to book editors, they should be a warning bell to writers, too. You may be safe during the honeymoon period, but once the editorial blood starts flowing, you should be polishing up proposals and outlines for general submission because there's a better-than-average chance that your option will be declined.

I know that these horror stories of publishing calamities are disheartening, but keep in mind the popular wisdom that whenever one door closes, another opens. I have found this to be especially true in publishing.

CHAPTER NINETEEN

A CHECKLIST FOR YOUR CAREER

As you have seen, the agent/author relationship is very important to the overall success of a writer's career. In today's publishing market, it's often more important than the relationship between the editor and the writer.

Finding an agent is a difficult task. Working with the agent you've found is also something you and your agent have to negotiate over time if the relationship is to be truly successful and rewarding for both of you. Although there is a general pattern to the way I work, each of my relationships with my clients is different and personal. So if you asked one of my clients what it was like to work with me, it might be a completely different experience for you than it is for him.

With that understood, there are basic skills and relationship expectations that your agent should satisfy for you. If you feel that any of them are being seriously fumbled, you should talk to your agent about them, unless they are so serious that you have already decided to leave.

AGENT/AUTHOR BASICS

1. You feel confident that you can always reach your agent, and that she will get back to you within twenty-four to forty-eight hours if it's necessary. When I attend writer's conferences, I am always asked, "Why doesn't my agent return my phone calls?" or "How long should I wait to hear from my agent?"

If the agent in question has agreed to represent you and is

not merely someone you hope *might* represent you, this is a legitimate gripe. Your agent should get back to you regarding any questions or information you might have about submissions, contracts, rights sales, possible future books and even writerly gossip that you've heard. However, if your agent has not gotten back to you because you've sent something to her to read, it's probably because she hasn't read it yet. Sometimes she'll have her assistant call you back, or she'll leave you a phone message or an E-mail.

As I've stated before, the agent workload is often colossal. Sometimes we have five existing clients in crisis mode and a major submission going to auction. There's often not a lot of time to get back to someone immediately for handholding, but we do manage to return *important* phone calls.

Sometimes your agent has an exceptionally hectic personal life and can't get to things as quickly as you would like. A good agent will clue you in to this before it happens (if she's going in for elective surgery, going on vacation or there's an illness in her family) or when it happens. You should be understanding, if this is not a permanent condition. If you're going to be working with someone for a long time, you both will have life crises and joys that will slow you down occasionally.

Sometimes it seems as though your agent is never in the office. Most good agents will tell you what their hours are, but you can't expect to reach your agent during nonbusiness hours. A lot of agents take a weekly reading day when they're not in the office (Fridays tend to be the day of choice), and they prefer not to do regular business on that day so that they can catch up with their reading workload. If there's a real catastrophe or someone makes an offer on your book they will get back to you, but otherwise they will get back to you on Monday.

2. Your agent responds to your work in a timely manner. This is a hard issue to grapple with, because most writers feel that their agents and editors just don't get back to them quickly enough. Even though they know that there are other clients, they still feel that *their* work should take priority.

If you've sent your agent a brief amount of work (a proposal or three chapters), he should get back to you in two weeks, unless he's out of town or in a crisis of his own. However, full manuscripts are hard to budget the time for, and as long as he lets you know that your work is on his schedule, he is doing his job.

If you've sent your agent more than one proposal or manuscript because you're anxious to get multiple-book deals, he will most likely look at one thing at a time.

Sometimes there's a system or schedule he's working under that puts your book on the back burner, such as the fact that he's already selling one vampire novel and wants to place that novel before he sends yours out. Although this might not be what you want to hear, he's justified in saying that he can't send them both out at the same time, so he wants to wait until the first one places to read yours.

3. Your agent knows the genre you're writing in. This is extremely important to your career. Having an agent who isn't well read in a genre you're writing in makes it much harder to place your work. You may think your work is being taken seriously, only to find out that your novel is resoundingly rejected because it has the same plot as one of Danielle Steel's novels but your agent hadn't read Steel, so both you and she didn't know that. (Of course, *you* should know your genre, too.)

If she's well-read in your genre, she may also be able to tell you that something in your novel will just not sell, such as the fact that it's set in a prison or that young adult books rarely deal with teen suicide, and you can make changes before the book goes out.

4. Your agent has a good reputation in the field, and she has good contacts. This applies to knowing your genre well, too. If your agent is respected by the editors in your genre, your work will be read quicker than the work of other agents who do not have such a reputation. If he knows the tastes of individual editors, what they're buying and how much he can expect the book to go for, you're way ahead of the game from the beginning.

If you ask editors about your agent, you may be surprised that they have less-than-glowing things to say about him. But the important thing is whether or not they respect him.

One editor I've done a lot of business with told a friend of a client that she thinks I am a horrible agent. When he asked why, she told him it was because I once broke a contract (at another publishing house with another editor). She thinks this is a crime. I disagree. I've only done this five times in my career, but sometimes it has to be done to protect the author. I am, after all, an author's representative, not an editor's friend. Although I think of myself as a fairly easygoing agent, there is now one editor who lives in fear that I will one day break a contract with her, so she treats me with a cautious respect that can only benefit my clients.

Your agent must also have good business contacts, and what I mean by this is agents in foreign countries as well as Hollywood agents.

5. Your agent gets your work out there. If your agent tells you that your work is on submission, it should be on submission. Unless it's an option or an exclusive, that means there should be three copies of your novel making the rounds, and five to ten copies of your nonfiction proposal being looked at. She should also follow up the submissions on a regular basis.

If you've sent your agent a number of projects and they're all in the same genre, she won't be able to send them all out at the same time. She has to give editors the chance to turn down one book before she sends them another one by the same author.

She may also tell you that she has another project out with the same group of editors that your work will be going to, so she has to wait a while before sending your material out.

However, there are also certain times of the year when your agent may decide to hold back on a project. These are the Thanksgiving to New Year's slowdown and the months of July and August, when everything in the business takes longer. The few times I've submitted material at this time (because I allowed an author's enthusiasm or financial need to sway me from what I know would be best for his book), I've always regretted it.

6. Your agent has the time to give you solid career planning advice and feedback. You have to decide what you want from your career, and you should be reevaluating where you are with every contract that you sign. It's not your agent's job to tell you where you should be headed, although he may have some suggestions for your career.

You should be comfortable with bouncing ideas off of your agent, and he should give you honest, thoughtful reactions to your book concepts and career goals. You should listen to your agent because he does have a wider perspective on the publishing industry, but ultimately you have to trust your own judgment.

The one thing I would recommend is that you never write a book you don't want to write or a book that you will be embarrassed about later on in your career, even if your agent and editor think it will be an instant best-seller. To thine own self be true. Although neither one of them will be happy with your decision, they should continue to respect you. After all, it's only one book in their publishing career (they can get someone else to write it if it's such a great idea), and they will have hundreds, if not thousands, of books under their belts, whereas you will have many fewer.

7. You feel that your agent understands your needs. Your agent can't understand your needs if you don't tell her what they are. Some authors are hesitant to say that they want to write full time in two years so they'd like concurrent multiple-book contracts or that they need extra money this year because their oldest daughter is getting married. They just cross their fingers and hope that this year will be better than the last one.

I have been successful in getting extra book contracts for every author who has told me that he needed it for a reason in the future (not within a week). Sometimes the writing jobs haven't been as fulfilling as what he wanted, but a good agent can usually get you the work if you tell him ahead of time.

Sometimes my authors have told me that even though they are very successful in their nonfiction field, what they really want to do is write fiction. It's hard for someone making $100,000 a book to realize that they may have to start all over again with fiction and get an advance as low as $5,000. (They may get more because of the success of their nonfiction books, but you can't count on that.) Once we've established this, I'm willing to work with them to get the novel into shape. Often this means relearning the craft of writing, because fiction takes different crafting skills than nonfiction. This can also be hard on the ego of someone who is a successful writer in another arena, but if they're willing to do the work, I'm willing to do my part.

Sometimes a successful genre novelist will tell me he wants to write a more commercial out-of-genre novel or a literary novel or that he wants to go from mass market to hardcover. If the book has promise, I'll work with him to get it to the level he wants. There's no guarantee that we will succeed, but I always give it my best shot.

8. Your agent should believe in you as a writer for the long term. I know of a literary agent who changes writers as often as she changes the color of her nail polish. She would sell a book for a lot of money, and if the book didn't earn out (which it usually didn't), the writer's option would be declined—and his career would be close to over. He would go to another agent, who would have to grow his career from the ground up if he could.

I vowed that I didn't want to be that kind of agent. I want to work with my authors for the long haul, and I want to see their careers grow with mine.

Now this may sound good if you have no book contract, but the downside to this is that an agent who wants to work with you for the long term will be thinking about whether or not your book will earn out. With this in mind, it's not the best thing in the world to get so much money for the book that your sales are disappointing. Even if the book sells 60,000 copies in hardcover, if the publisher paid $250,000 for the book, that's a disaster for them.

Although I have never turned down a large advance, there's a point at which I start growing nervous for my authors. We had one situation where a twenty-four-year-old first-time author had been offered $200,000. We had another house interested in him, and we could have gotten more money, but this was the high reaches of what we could expect these novels to earn, and we didn't want him to be a one- or two-book wonder, so we told him that this was enough money from the best editor for his book.

On another first book I sold, I was told by another agent that I could have gotten much more for it. I knew that this book alone had changed the author's tax bracket and that too much more would go directly to the IRS. The book earned out, and eventually earned the additional money that the other agent had said it would (over four years), but as far as the publishing industry was concerned my author was a glowing success. We used her strong sales figures to get book contracts over the next ten years that earned her more than a million dollars. I doubt that she would have had as long a career if we had started at advances that were too high for the books.

9. Your relationship with your agent is an honest one. If you don't trust your agent or you can't tell your agent what's on your mind, your relationship is doomed. Just as you have to be honest with your lawyer and your accountant, you have to tell your agent what she needs to know.

You also have to be comfortable enough with her that you can tell her if there's something that's not working. This doesn't necessarily mean that the relationship has to end. Perhaps the two of you can work out a compromise that will improve the relationship.

After representing one of my authors for a few books, she called me and asked me if she could discuss something that was bothering her. She said that my unbridled enthusiasm for her work and my detailed plans for where I thought I was going to sell it were great, but when things didn't work out, she felt depressed and disappointed. I realized that, for her, it was not the best thing for me to say I was going to sell the work here or there, but just to tell her that I would send it out right away with enormous enthusiasm. I also explained to her that in order for me to send the work out, I had to believe that it would sell to that editor, publisher or magazine. We've worked together for years since then, and I have kept this in mind in dealing with other authors as well. Her thoughtful comment has actually made me a better agent.

10. You genuinely like and respect your agent, and you feel that he feels the same way about you. You don't have to *love* your agent, but you should like and respect him as a person, not just as an agent. This will make it easier for you to bring up tough subjects and to feel that you deserve some of his time.

Some authors choose an agent because they're high-powered in the publishing industry. They are impressed by what he's done for some big-name author and expect the same thing. But if they don't have the same kind of high-profile career as the established author, they will be second- or third-tier authors on his list.

Some agents have a reputation for tenacity and even bitchiness, which can be great for dealing with publishers, but it's not wonderful when it's aimed at the writer. It's hard to maintain a relationship with someone who's always telling you your work is not good enough or that it could always be better, or that he's doing you a favor by representing you.

If there's something about your agent that you really don't like and respect (he once told you that romance novels were stupid, and you secretly want to write romance novels), the relationship is going to unravel someday. Try to find someone you would feel comfortable inviting to your family gatherings as well as business meetings. Your agent is your writing partner, and you should never have a partner you can't trust and respect.

CHAPTER TWENTY

CHANGING AGENTS

How to Do It Right When the Relationship's Not Working

I've told you about all of my successful relationships with my authors, but this is the chapter where I share my less-than-perfect experiences.

Every agent has been left by an author. It's one of the sad and difficult parts of the job, but it's also something we all understand comes with the territory. Sometimes things just don't work out right.

However, this doesn't have to be a hurtful screaming match or even a distant so-long and goodbye. If you have any respect for what the agent did for you, take the time to end this relationship as painlessly and professionally as possible.

Keep in mind that if your agent did sell a book or two for you, she will continue to be the agent of record on that book, and all revenue and subrights sales of the book will continue to flow through her office. Therefore, it's in your best interest to make her want to take your calls if you have to call again. Your new agent may not want to follow up on business that has nothing to do with her or that she doesn't make any money from.

The best way to end the author/agent relationship is in person. You don't have to take your agent out to lunch to do this, but you should at least do it over the phone. You want to give your agent an opportunity to discuss the reasons why you are leaving and perhaps straighten things out if there is a misunderstanding.

If the relationship has deteriorated to the point where it's antagonistic or you feel you really don't want to do this over the phone, the next best way to do it is to write a short but informative letter, with an invitation for the agent to call you if she'd like to discuss it. If you have no intention of talking to her and won't be answering the phone for the next few days, don't include the invitation.

Here is a sample letter of how to end the author/agent relationship.

> Dear Lori:
>
> I've enjoyed working with you over the past years, and I appreciate all the sales you've brought me. However, I've been feeling for a while that our career paths are going in different directions, and I feel it's time for me to look elsewhere for representation.
>
> If you'd like to discuss this, please feel free to call me at home.

Never fax this kind of letter to your agent's office. The office is a public work area, and your agent may not want her assistants or colleagues to know that you're leaving her before she does. Send the letter with the words *Personal and Confidential* written prominently on the outside of the envelope. It's best to do this by regular mail, but if you can't wait you can send it overnight. It goes without saying that you shouldn't use E-mail for this kind of communication.

If you signed an agency agreement, you should follow the terms laid out in that contract. You make have to give your agent a thirty- or ninety-day notice, and you may have to wait for her to finish any pending business. It's never a good idea to ask an agent to pull a book from submission (it makes you look bad to the editors), so try to do this before the next book goes out.

Of course, there may be more that you want to say than what is in the letter above, but remember that putting hurtful things on paper is not the most professional way to do things. Sometimes there's so much ego involved that it's only after the dust has settled that you realize it was just time to move on for both of you and not really anybody's fault.

Sometimes it is somebody's fault. There are legitimate reasons to leave an agent, such as lack of communication, failure to pay you your money on time and failure to get your work out promptly and to follow up on submissions. If there are no extenuating circumstances on your agent's part (some personal or professional crisis that she neglected to tell you about), you have justifiable reason to leave.

Most of the time it's not as cut and dried as that. Sometimes you feel you have to leave your agent because she no longer has the right enthusiasm for your work. She'll send it on to the editor who bought the last book, but if your option is declined she'll tell you to try something else for that editor instead of sending the work you've already done to a handful of other editors.

Sometimes agents get lazy. As their clients get more successful, they don't want to send out as many copies of a book as they had to when everyone was starting out. They like doing business with a handful of editors and want to keep doing business that way. I know of one agent who sells all her books to five editors. If the five editors she does business with don't want to publish your work, you may be right in looking for an agent who submits to a broader range of editors.

Sometimes an agent really doesn't like the book you've asked her to represent. This is a touchy situation, especially if it's a departure from what you've been writing for the past few years.

Just as I recommend that authors must be true to their real selves, agents have to do the same. Our reputation goes out with every book we send out. I will not submit a book that I think is flawed or bad. I'll tell my author why, and if he insists that the book must go out, we will probably part company.

This *has* happened to me. In one instance an author had basically written the same book three times, and I was getting tired of reading it. His editor had turned down his option, and instead of writing a new book he had labored over polishing this rather hackneyed book idea. When he sent the revised version of this novel to me, I told him that it still didn't work for me and that he should try something different. He insisted it was brilliant (and it might have been the first time around) and he left, looking for another agent.

The postscript to this story is that I had told him that I did like his early work, and that if he ever came up with something different I'd be willing to take a look at it. He called me about five years later, upset that I hadn't responded to a letter he had sent me a month before that. Unbeknownst to me, he had changed his name back to his real name (he had been writing under a pseudonym), so I had no idea who he was when the letter came in. My assistant didn't recognize his name either, and the letter was put into the pile of unsolicited manuscripts we get.

I called him back and told him to send what he had written. He told me he needed a quick reaction because there was a timeliness to the book. I told him I was leaving for a three-week vacation in days, and that I wouldn't be able to get to it for at least a month. When I came back from vacation, there was a hostile message saying that since he hadn't heard from me, he would have to assume I wasn't interested. I sent the book back unread.

I had another falling out with a client I had represented for about six years. Her career had grown during that time to the point where she was now a full-time writer with multiple book contracts in two separate genres. Out of the blue she sent me something completely different from what she had been publishing, and it was not in a genre I knew at all. I read it and was not impressed. It did absolutely nothing for me.

When I have a client who insists upon writing in a genre or area I don't know or understand, what I often do is ask another agent in that genre to take a look at the material for me. Eight agents share my office space now, so there's always someone I can consult with whose judgment I trust. If they really like the book, sometimes I let them handle the author for that particular genre (such as children's books, which I know nothing about).

I had a good friend who worked in children's books, so I asked her to give the partial manuscript a read. She told me it was unsalable. When I told this to the author, she insisted that I send it to her editor anyway. Her editor *did* buy books in this area, so I sent it to her. She avoided my calls for a few weeks, and then sent it back to me with a terse letter saying "Not for us."

When I told this to the author, she insisted that I send the partial manuscript out on a wider submission, but I had to tell her that I just didn't believe I could sell it. I loved her other work and thought that she should grow in those directions, but she felt that she had to try this new direction—and we parted company. Again, I told her that I would always take her calls.

She had many agents over the next few years, but we're now working together again.

Sometimes your agent just can't sell a book, no matter how much she loves it. I actually went after an author because I loved some work of his that I had seen. When he called, I took him on right away, and we sold his first novel at auction for a nice sum of money. The book didn't do particularly well, but we received excellent reviews and quotes, and everyone who read this kind of book knew about it.

One of the reasons his book didn't do particularly well was that his editor left publishing and the line of books she started was dropped, so the publisher declined his option. I went to the underbidder, but the market had changed, and that editor soon left his publisher, too.

My author's second novel was brilliant and dark, just like his first one, but I couldn't find a single editor who saw it the way I did. I must have sent the novel to twenty-five editors over two years, but I just couldn't find a home for it. The same thing happened with his British agent.

He did write a partial manuscript for another novel, but it was tied to a centennial event, and there were other books coming into the marketplace that competed with it, so I couldn't place that either. He even tried his hand at nonfiction, but he chose to write something on music instead of film (where he had an extensive background), and the editors just didn't think his credentials were strong enough in that area.

When he told me he thought it was time to try another agent, I could see his point. It had been two years since I had sold anything for him. But I felt really bad, even though I knew I had done everything I knew how to do. I'm also sure he will go on to great things—and I hope he'll remember me.

Sometimes the market crashes on an author, and he thinks it's his agent's fault, or that a bigger agent will be able to get him through lean times better. When the horror market crashed, many of the horror writers I had been working with for years left me and signed up with other agents, but most of them ended up going without contracts for years.

When the horror bust came, I told all my horror authors to start writing young adult horror (the *Goosebumps* phenomenon was just taking off) or to try another genre like dark fantasy or mystery. Many of them didn't want to believe that they couldn't publish horror any more, because they had written some really good books that would have to be put aside. They thought the problem was me.

Sometimes authors leave agents because they think they need to be with a bigshot agent or agency to get the big money that they think everyone else is getting. I had one twenty-six-year-old author whose proposal I had worked on extensively (I copyedited the whole thing), and I got him $60,000 for his first book. We did have another publisher interested in the book who told us to name our price, but the editor wanted a different book from the one the author wanted to write. We went with the $60,000 offer because the first editor really understood the book, and I knew she would work well with the author.

Soon after the book was delivered, my author started sending me clips about $500,000 advances for books written by people under thirty. He was now on a local radio show and was certain he was going to be the next Charles Osgood. He started sending me ideas for big-political-issue books, when his first book had been extremely personal. He had an idea for a wonderful personal book, which I thought I could place as an article in one of the men's magazines and then sell as a book. He wanted his next book to be really big, so he left me and went to one of the big agencies.

The editor who had bought his personal book turned down his sweeping social commentary. His new agent didn't really know how to sell him, and one day called his editor and asked her to give her a $500,000 idea for him. The editor told her that if she had a $500,000 idea, she'd write the book herself.

Occasionally agents fire clients, but this doesn't happen very often. I had a lawyer for a client who was never happy with my work. He wanted lots of money for his book, and when it went to auction, we got what the market would bear, which wasn't bad. As soon as I sold the book, he wanted to know what else I was going to do for him, and he even commented that he didn't think he needed an agent anymore. He also had a writing partner who was driving me crazy trying to get me to resell old book ideas, so I finally told the two of them to find someone else to work with.

It turns out that he was dissatisfied with everyone, from his editor to his publisher to his writing partner. Luckily I stepped back when I did, because he sued his publisher for failure to make him a household word, and I would certainly have been party to that suit if I had continued to represent him.

I really believe in the African-American saying "God don't like ugly," as well as "What comes around, goes around," and I find this is especially true in the publishing universe. There's a fairly well-known story about an author who left his agent in a disrespectful way, and a decade later his life is still in tatters.

A famous foreign writer came to New York and stayed with his agent, a well-respected 1960s radical. While in New York, he surreptitiously met with an agent we in the business like to think of as the devil incarnate and decided to leave the agent who had guided his career for years. He told her the news on the last day of his trip. Satan managed to get him a wonderful new deal, but the consequences of it were that he was unable to be seen in public for most of the last decade. God don't like ugly.

One of my agent partners recently took on a client who felt that her agent just didn't respect the kind of books she was writing. She was an astrologer and had spent hours drafting the right language for this letter. She finally came up with the phrase "Our karma has ended," which I think is particularly appropriate for this kind of book. The day she mailed her letter, she received a fax from her agent saying that he thought their relationship was just not working. Talk about kismet.

EPILOGUE
Even Agents Need Agents

Even though I consider myself a professional writer and I've worked in publishing for fifteen years, when I put on my writer's hat I become as anxious and insecure as any other writer. When you send your work out a little piece of yourself goes out there with it, and any rejection feels like rejection of you. You just can't be objective when someone doesn't like something you've written.

This book came about because I had an agent. I would not be writing it if it wasn't for the calm, level-headed guidance of my agent.

I wanted to write a book on etiquette for writers because I had a brief period of time where many of my established writers seemed to all have their planetary influences in stupidity. What I mean by this is that a number of authors who should have known better did a whole bunch of really self-destructive things to their writing careers. When I calmed down enough to explain to them that you don't bring your new boyfriend or your seventeen-year-old son to your editorial lunches, they said that no one had ever told them that. So I thought a book laying out exactly what writers should and shouldn't do would find an audience.

My agent thought it was a good idea, too, so he encouraged

me to prepare a proposal. He pitched it to a lot of editors who were signing up etiquette books, as well as editors who edited writing books. Some thought it was too small a book; others thought I should do a big book on publishing etiquette in general.

An editor at Writer's Digest Books received the idea for my book very enthusiastically, but when he brought it up to his editorial board, he learned that they had recently published a book on this subject, and that it had been one of their weakest sellers. But he liked my work and voice and said he wanted to work with me.

My agent arranged for us to have a brainstorming conversation, during which the editor informed me that Writer's Digest Books was always looking for someone to write a book on agenting. They polled their reading audience every year, and this was always one of the books that the readers asked to see. He said he was familiar with my article in the *1994 Guide to Literary Agents*, and he thought I would be the perfect author for the book.

I was a little stunned, because I would never have thought enough of myself to pitch this idea on my own. Even though I had worked as an agent for fifteen years and had a few big professional accomplishments, I thought a publisher like Writer's Digest Books would seek out someone who was more of a celebrity agent. (Looking back, I realize that a celebrity agent wouldn't have written a book as honest as this one.)

So I wrote up a new proposal, and the editor got back to me fairly quickly. He told me that the book was slanted too much toward the already-published writer, and most of the Writer's Digest books were sold to new writers. He again emphasized that Writer's Digest Books wanted to publish a book on agenting.

I rewrote the proposal again, remembering that I was a fairly new book author myself, so it should be easy to identify with the readership. My agent also assured me that Writer's Digest was really interested in the book and that I wasn't just spinning my wheels. The editor called back with an enthusiastic reaction to the new proposal and then told us it would be another month before he got the green light, but that he was optimistic that the sale would go through.

As I said at the beginning of this epilogue, it's impossible to step back when it's your work. Without an agent overseeing this whole deal-making and negotiation process, I'm certain I would never have gotten this book contract. My ego would have gotten in my way.

With that proviso, I will now tell you the story of the agent who represented himself. It has a happy ending, but the middle of the story is gut-wrenching.

While my father was dying from cancer, my business partner decided to write a proposal for a how-to book on writing.
I've represented him for years, but now that he was an agent
and I was obviously distracted, he decided to represent himself
because I had said that I couldn't handle a large submission at
that time. I did suggest that he wait until my presence of mind
was better—but he wanted a book deal now! I didn't have the
emotional strength to argue.

Besides, he already had an editor who was interested in the
book. He had been working with an editor who published
both books and a magazine, and she had suggested that he
write the book in the first place. He wrote up a proposal, and
she made a small offer. I wanted him to try a bigger submission
process, but he wanted the deal, so he went ahead with it.

He negotiated his own contract, too. He just asked me to
look it over. Every time I pointed out areas where the deal
could be improved, he told me not to worry about it.

When he had finished the first draft of the book, he sent it
to his editor, and it was returned to him with corrections and
comments on every page. He felt as if his editors (there were
three of them) were telling him he couldn't write, and it badly
bruised his ego, especially since he had already published two
novels and had been a BBC journalist in England.

Writing nonfiction, especially a how-to book, is different

from writing fiction, and this was his first nonfiction book. His editors actually had good points to make, but they made them all wrong—and in red ink, too. They should have written him an editorial letter outlining the problems they had with the book, and then asked him to rework the material. Instead, he felt overwhelmed by pages of comments, some of which were sarcastic.

Even though I wasn't the agent on the book, I did look over their suggestions because he is my friend. When I translated them into coherent recommendations (your references are too arcane, there aren't enough female writers mentioned, and using contemporary American best-sellers as examples would make the book stronger), he was able to rewrite the book, but he resented it the whole time. When he complained that he couldn't find female writers to use as examples, I made suggestions for him (but I made him read their books, too).

By that time a lot of damage had already been done. He had alienated his editors by railing against their suggestions—and then grudgingly did what they asked. Since I wasn't handling the deal, I didn't intervene on the phone conversations and correspondence. And because my dad was dying, he didn't tell me about them until after the fact.

He did tell me that when he sent back the manuscript, he had included a letter saying that he wasn't prepared to do any more work on the book (a definite no-no, should you ever be so inclined, even though you are free to feel that way). A month or two went by and he heard nothing from his editor, except that the book was now scheduled for publication. The relationship between him and his editor had grown so icy that he finally asked me to call and see when he would be getting the copyedited manuscript or page proofs.

I called the editor and introduced myself, and she was unbelievably cold with me. She told me there would be no examining of either the copyedited manuscript or the page proofs because the author was too difficult to deal with.

He went ballistic, and I called back and said that they would have to let him see the page proofs, which is what most publishers do.

My father died that week, and I closed the office from the Wednesday he died until the Monday after the funeral, a total of three business days. I didn't check messages because I couldn't, but I did put a message on the answering machine saying that the office was closed due to a death in the family.

When we came back that Monday, there was a message on the machine informing us that the book had been cancelled. I called immediately, but the editor told me it was too late to change her mind. We should have called back sooner. I told her my father had just died. She told me she didn't care, but my partner could keep the money they had paid him because they weren't even interested in dealing with him again on a first proceeds sale.

My partner felt angry and depressed. He had told everyone he knew about the sale of this book, and now it wasn't going to be published—and he had already written it twice.

I felt terrible too, because I knew that I should have taken control of the situation. If I had insisted on being his agent on the book, I know that the cancellation would never have happened.

The next time around, he waited for me to grieve a bit. I was allowed to send the book out to a number of editors who knew his work, both as a writer and as an editor. One house had just recently started a series of how-to books for writers. They bought the book for a lot more money and launched their new line with it.

And his editor hardly touched the manuscript. She said it was just about perfect and that he had been a joy to work with.

APPENDIX

Suggested Reading

Elements of Style, William Strunk and E.B. White. The only grammar and language book you'll every need. Short and even fun to read. The essential book for every writer of both fiction and nonfiction.

How to Write Best-Selling Fiction, Dean Koontz. A gem of a book that is now out of print. You'll probably have to order it from the library, but Koontz's first-person account of how he transformed himself from a genre writer to a best-selling author is priceless. The material on the publishing market is out of date, but this is an accurate account of what publishing was like in the 1980s.

Bird by Bird: Some Instruction on Writing and Life, Anne Lamott. Another classic and the most inspirational writer's how-to book I've ever read (and I've read quite a few). As soon as I finished it, I started over again.

Elements of Story-Telling, Peter Rubie. The essential guide for rewriting. Rubie is an expert on structure and plotting, and he teaches the beginning writer how to restructure his work to make it stronger.

Dean Koontz: A Biography, Katherine Ramsland. An in-depth look at Koontz's writing career, from his childhood through his climb to the best-seller list.

Beyond the Bestseller and ***This Business of Publishing: An Insider's View of Current Trends and Tactics***, Richard Curtis. Richard Curtis has been a literary agent for more than thirty years and has been writing about the business for almost as long. *Beyond the Best-seller* is a collection of articles he wrote about the various aspects of the business from an agent's point of view. *This Business of Publishing* is his take on the publishing industry as we enter the twenty-first century.

The Complete Idiot's Guide to Getting Published, Sheree Bykofsky and Jennifer Basye Sander. A comprehensive basic guide to publishing by a literary agent and a book editor.

The Observation Deck: A Tool Kit for Writers, Naomi Epel. If you're the kind of writer who keeps a journal and/or likes flexing your writing muscles with exercises, this is a clever inspirational writer's kit.

Assorted Baby Names books such as ***Puffy, Xena, Uma and Quentin*** by Joal Ryan. Every writer of fiction should have at least one, if not three, baby names books on hands for help with naming characters.

Resources

GENERAL WRITERS ORGANIZATIONS

American Society of Journalists and Authors
1501 Broadway
New York NY 10036
(212) 997-0947

Author's Guild
330 West 42nd Street
New York NY 10036
(212) 563-5904
(212) 564-8363 (fax)

PEN American Center
568 Broadway
New York NY 10012
(212) 334-1660

National Writer's Union
13 Astor Place
New York NY 10003
(212) 254-0279

GENRE WRITERS ORGANIZATIONS

Horror Writers Association (HWA)
P.O. Box 50577
Palo Alto CA 94303

Mystery Writers of America (MWA)
17 East 47th Street 6th Floor
New York NY 10017
(212) 888-8171

Romance Writers of America (RWA)
13700 Veterans Memorial Drive, Suite 315
Houston TX 77014
(713) 440-6885

Science Fiction Writers of America (SFWA)
P.O. Box 171
Unity ME 04988-0171

Sisters in Crime
P.O. Box 442124
Lawrence KS 66044-8933
(785) 842-1325
sistersincrime@juno.com

Society of Children's Book Writers and Illustrators
345 North Maple Drive, Suite 296
Beverly Hills CA 90210
(310) 859-9887

Western Writers of America
1012 Fair Street
Franklin TN 37064
(615) 791-1444

OTHER ORGANIZATIONS AND PUBLICATIONS

Association of Author's Representatives (AAR)
10 Astor Plaza, 3rd Floor
New York NY 10003
(212) 353-3709

Publisher's Weekly (and Library Journal)
245 West 17th Street
New York NY 10011

Kirkus Review
200 Park Avenue South
New York NY 10003
(212) 777-4554

Literary Market Place (LMP)
R.R. Bowker
121 Chanlon Road
New Providence NJ 07094
888-BOWKER2 (to order)

Collaboration Agreement

This is a blank collaboration agreement, which we use when two or more authors are brought together to work on a book. It can be used with a celebrity or expert and a writer, as well as with two writers of fiction.

The collaboration agreement lays out the terms of the partnership, as well as foreseeing most of the problems that can come up between authors.

Agreement made this first day of _____ 1999, among _____ and _____

% Perkins, Rubie Associates
240 West 35 St.
Suite 500
New York NY 10001

In consideration of mutual convenants hereinafter set forth, the parties hereto agree as follows:

1. This Agreement and all the terms and conditions enumerated herein shall encompass the United States of America, its territories and possessions and all foreign countries.

2. The Authors mutually agree to collaborate in the development of a nonfiction book about _____
The credit lines shall read: by _____

3. The Authors shall jointly and exclusively own and hold the literary property rights, their residual rights, subsidiary rights and all copyrights.

4. Neither Author shall make any contract with a third party in

connection with this literary property or any literary property which will abrogate the rights of the other or interfere with or limit in any way the sale of the literary properties under this Agreement.

5. This Agreement may not be assigned or transferred, except to the extent that the parties hereto may assign or transfer any monies due them respectively.

6. The Authors agree to work together and cooperate with each other to the best of their abilities to produce the manuscripts(s).

It is agreed and understood that _____ may take on additional contracts during the course of writing this book. However, she will ensure that all deadlines are met. The parties hereto agree not to participate in the writing or publication of any book that would directly compete with this property or otherwise adversely affect sales of the books.

7. Perkins, Rubie Associates is the authorized agent for the Authors in connection with negotiations regarding the literary property, their residual and subsidiary rights, including but not limited to first serial, electronic, foreign, translation, dramatic and audio rights. Agent agrees to consult with the authors before accepting any offers or licenses on their behalf.

8. All monies, income, property, fees and royalties derived from the literary properties, their publication, residual rights and subsidiary rights, including but not limited to those outlined in paragraph 7, shall be distributed as follows:

>The agent will receive a commission of fifteen percent (15%) of gross earnings for the above mentioned rights, and twenty percent (20%) of the gross earnings on foreign rights. The remainder, which is the property of the authors, will be divided as follows: _____% to _____ and _____% to _____.

9. "Gross earnings" shall mean one hundred percent of all monies, earnings and royalties of any kind.

10. Authors represent and warrant that they have the full power and authority to enter into this Agreement and that neither they nor any of the literary properties under this Agreement will be subject to any other commitments which would conflict or interfere with the performance of the Agents' services hereunder. Authors shall indemnify the Agent and hold him harmless from and against any claim, action, proceeding, damage or expense (including counsel fees) which Authors may suffer as a result of or in connection with any breach or alleged breach.

11. This Agreement cannot be amended, except by written notice executed by all parties.

12. In the event, notwithstanding this Agreement, should any party hereto breach the terms thereof, then the proceeds derived from said breach shall be held against that party in trust and as trust funds for the use and benefit of the other contracting parties in the proportions herein provided.

13. The Parties agree to settle any negotiation, claim or dispute arising out of or in connection with this Agreement or breach thereof in the City of New York with the then rules of the American Arbitration Association, and such judgment may be entered in any court having jurisdiction thereof.

14. Regardless of the place of its physical execution, this Agreement shall be interpreted under the laws of the State of New York and of the United States of America.

15. In witness Whereof the parties have executed this Agreement the day and year first above written in triplicate original

counterparts, each of which shall consititute an original.

AGREED AND ACCEPTED:

PERKINS, RUBIE ASSOCIATES

_____

_____   _____

Deal Memo

Peter Rubie and I developed this deal memo as a checklist for deal points when we negotiate a book sale. It is a shorthand account of the areas in a publisher's contract where there is room for negotiation. Use it as a reference in conjunction with chapter twelve.

BOOK TITLE: _____

AUTHOR: _____

PUBLISHER/EDITOR: _____

ROYALTY/ADVANCE: $ _____

□ ½ signing _____   □ ½ signing or $ _____

□ ½ on D&A of ms. _____   □ _____ on D&A of an outline

□ _____ other   □ _____ on D&A of a ms.

Book #1   **Book #2**   **Book #3**

□ on D&A of an outline   □ on D&A of an outline   □ on D&A of an outline

□ on D&A of a ms.   □ on D&A of a ms.   □ on D&A of a ms.

□ Option: Sample chapter and outline _____

Territory

□ North America   □ World English   □ World

Royalties (on retail price):

□ Hardcover 10%/ 12½%/ 15% (on 1st 5,000, 2nd 5,000, thereafter) _____

□ Trade 7½% or _____

□ Mass market 8% or _____

□ Electronic 10% or _____

☐ Escalators: "_____" up to "_____,ooo" then "_____" after

☐ Best-seller bonus

Pass Through on subsidiary rights

☐ Split cost of indexing between author and publisher

☐ Reversion of Publisher rights after 18 months if nothing happens ☐ Yes ☐ No

☐ We keep Dramatic: ☐ Yes ☐ No

☐ We keep Audio: ☐ Abridged ☐ Unabridged   ☐ Yes ☐ No

☐ We keep Electronic other than verbatim reproduction: ☐ Yes ☐ No

☐ We sell rights: ☐ Yes ☐ No

☐ Book Clubs 50/50

☐ 1st Serial   90/10 or _____

☐ 2nd Serial   60/40 or _____

☐ We keep Merchandising   ☐ Yes ☐ No

Other Rights We Get

☐ Author consultation on manuscript, cover copy and cover design

☐ Publish within 18 months or _____

☐ 20 copies to author, 10 to the agent

☐ Author has right to retain own legal counsel

☐ No joint accounting

Nonfiction Proposal

This is the proposal I used to sell *The Science of Star Wars* by Jeanne Cavelos, which was published by St. Martin's Press in hardcover in May of 1999.

This book was created over a lunch with the St. Martin's editor, who was interested in publishing a more serious Star Wars book to tie in with the release of the new movie. The editor had originally envisioned it as a trade paperback, but when I told him that Cavelos, who had been an astrophysicist at NASA, might be interested in writing the book, the parameters changed slightly.

Because this was a proposal for a specific editor and we were under the gun to get under contract, this proposal is collapsed, but you will see that other than the lack of a full marketing section, all the basic ingredients of a proposal are here.

THE SCIENCE OF STAR WARS
Jeanne Cavelos

"A long time ago in a galaxy far, far away . . ."

Words that sound more like the opening to a fairy tale than to a science fiction saga. And in many ways *Star Wars* feels like fantasy, with the mystical power of the Force; great wizards, called Jedi Knights, who wield it; and great powers of good and evil locked in an epic battle.

Yet *Star Wars* also contains spaceships, aliens, bizarre planets and high-tech weapons—all the trappings of science fiction. This blend makes the fantastic seem more plausible because of its grounding in science. Yet how realistic, how possible, is this galaxy far, far away?

"It's the ship that made the Kessel Run
in less than twelve parsecs."

Han Solo's boast is perhaps the most glaring scientific error in the *Star Wars* films. Since the parsec is a unit of distance, Han is bragging, in essence, that he got to Kessel in twelve miles. Not terribly impressive, if it's twelve miles from here to Kessel.

But the purpose of this book is not to nitpick. In creating the part science fiction/part fantasy/part myth that is *Star Wars*, George Lucas did not seek to create a scientifically accurate futuristic universe. He sought to combine elements from many different sources and alchemize them into something completely new. And he succeeded.

Yet shining the light of science on the *Star Wars* universe can provide us with some fascinating insights, and can allow us to see these brilliant works from a new perspective. Wouldn't you like to know . . .

- Could a weapon be built with enough power to destroy an entire planet? How close are we to such technology?
- Could a life-supporting planet like Tatooine circle two suns?
- Could light sabers possibly be built, and how would they work?
- How might spaceships like the *Millennium Falcon* make the exhilarating jump into hyperspace?
- Might we access a force with our minds to move objects and communicate telepathically with each other?
- How close are we to creating sophisticated robots like C-3PO and R2-D2, and will robots of the future act as emotional as this distinctive pair?
- Why do Jawas' eyes glow?
- How might speeders and other antigravitational transports operate?

Drawing on the latest scientific discoveries and research, and interviewing the foremost experts in these disciplines, Jeanne Cavelos will explore the answers to these questions.

A preliminary table of contents includes the following:

(1) *Planetary Environments:* Are planets as common as

they seem in *Star Wars*? How likely are Earth-type planets? Is it likely that a planet would be entirely desert (Tatooine), entirely snow covered (Hoth) or entirely forested (Endor and the moon of Yavin)? What effect would the twin suns of Tatooine have on the planet? How might farming be carried out there? What are conditions really like within an asteroid field, and what are the chances of successfully navigating one? Is life likely on a moon, such as the Ewok moon of Endor? Could humans survive without artificial aids on many different planets?

(2) *Aliens:* What might alien life be like? How likely are we to find humanoid aliens? How likely are the various aliens shown, from Chewbacca to Greedo to Yoda to Jabba the Hut to the trash compactor's slime snake? What types of environments might they have come from? In cases where we know an alien's planet of origin, is it likely that such a creature would have evolved in that environment? What types of creatures would we expect to develop in the various environments shown in *Star Wars*? Could giant slugs live inside asteroids? Can Ewoks really climb trees?

(3) *Space Ships:* If we are to believe Han Solo's claim that the *Millenium Falcon* can "make point five past light speed," how might ships some day be able to travel faster than the speed of light? Can any current scientific theories help explain this? How might hyperdrive work? What is hyperspace? Could wormholes be used to travel rapidly from one star to another? Is it likely that space ships of the future will have their hulls covered with the messy-looking outer mechanisms characteristic of most *Star Wars* ships? How might the artificial gravity of the ships be generated? Could *Star Wars* ships accelerate rapidly without crushing their passengers? Can we possibly offer any scientific explanation that would make Han Solo's infamous claim about the Kessel Run as impressive as he thinks it is? And what about the biggest ship of them all, the Death Star? Can current science explain how a planet-killing weapon might some day be created?

(4) ***Droids and Other Technological Marvels:*** How ad-

vanced are the robots being built today? Might robots like R2-D2 and C-3PO someday be within our reach? Are robots of the future likely to be similar to the robots depicted in *Star Wars*? Could we someday build robots as intelligent as Artoo and Threepio? Can we make robots that see, hear and speak? Can we create robots that have their own emotions, and why would we want to? Why do Artoo and Threepio constantly argue? Can we create bionic limbs like Vader's and Luke's? Are the AT-AT Walkers practical all-terrain armored vehicles? Will we be able to make blasters like the one Han Solo carries? How might a light saber work? Could a city be built to hover in the clouds? Would it work the same way as Luke's speeder? How about those neat flying cycles in the forest of Endor?

(5) *The Force:* A necessarily more speculative chapter. Do today's top scientists believe it likely, or even possible, that a previously undiscovered force connecting everything might someday be discovered? What might the qualities of such a force be? Is there any evidence of such a force? Is there any way to incorporate "the Force" into our current scientific understanding of the universe? Can the Force be explained by quantum theory? How could Jedi affect such a force with their minds? Can the mind control events on the quantum level? Do humans have any psychic abilities? What evidence have scientists found of telepathy, clairvoyance and psychokinesis?

These topics will be covered in an engaging, lively manner that an audience with only a minimal science background can understand. Constant references to the movies will keep fans involved and fascinated, while current, cutting-edge research grounds the book in science and reveals incredible discoveries that may some day lead us into a *Star Wars* future. Sidebars will break up the text with interesting asides. The book will be approximately 90,000 words.

Star Wars has become a classic series of movies, among the top-grossing films of all time, and has generated a best-selling series of books. With the release of a new trilogy of films beginning in 1999, excitement about all things *Star Wars* is sure to reach a new high. Books like *The Physics of Star Trek* by

Lawrence Krauss have found phenomenal success in exploring the science behind science fiction. Yet no such book has been done about *Star Wars*. The *Star Wars* films have a phenomenally loyal and passionate fan following. They'll find *The Science of Star Wars* an illuminating must-read that adds a new dimension to their favorite movies and reveals amazing scientific discoveries actually being made today.

ABOUT THE AUTHOR

Jeanne Cavelos is a writer, scientist, editor and teacher—but first and foremost, a *Star Wars* fan. She saw *Star Wars* when it first came out in 1977, when she was 17. The opening shot, in which a huge star destroyer flew endlessly out of the screen, sent her heart racing. The *Star Wars* films fueled Jeanne's interest in space exploration and the possibility of alien life.

Jeanne began her professional life as an astrophysicist and mathematician, teaching astronomy at Michigan State University and Cornell University, and working in the Astronaut Training Division at NASA's Johnson Space Center.

Her love of science fiction led her to earn her MFA in creative writing. She moved into publishing, becoming a senior editor at Dell Publishing, where she ran the science fiction/fantasy program and crafted the Abyss horror line, for which she won the World Fantasy Award. In her eight years in New York publishing, she edited numerous award-winning and best-selling authors' books.

A few years ago, she left New York to pursue her own writing career. She is the author of *The Science of the X-Files*, coming from Berkley/Boulevard in 11/98, and the *Babylon 5* novel *The Shadow Within* (Dell, 4/97), which has been called "one of the best TV tie-in novels ever written" (*Dreamwatch* magazine). Other recent works include a novella, "Negative Space," in the science fiction anthology *Decalog 5: Wonders* (Virgin Publishing) and a chapter, "Innovation in Horror," in *Writing Horror: A Handbook by the Horror Writers Association* (Writer's Digest Books). She has published short fiction, articles and essays in a number of magazines, and is a regular book reviewer for *Realms of Fantasy* magazine.

As an editor, she runs Jeanne Cavelos Editorial Services, a full-service freelance company that provides editing, ghost-writing, consulting and critiquing services. Among its clients are major publishers and best-selling writers.

Since she loves working with developing writers, Jeanne created and serves as director of Odyssey, an annual six-week summer workshop for writers of fantasy, science fiction and horror held at New Hampshire College in Manchester. Writers come from all across the United States and Canada to focus on their craft and receive detailed, in-depth feedback on their work. Jeanne is also an English lecturer at Saint Anselm College in Manchester, New Hampshire.

Fiction Proposal

I used this proposal to sell Chris Golden's dark fantasy thriller, *Strangewood*, which will be published by NAL in the fall of 1999. Peter Straub gave the author a quote, which is on the cover of the novel.

Golden is an established author in the horror and young adult fields, but this was his first dark fantasy novel. We sent it out as a blind submission, meaning the editor did not know the identity of the writer until she called to make an offer.

STRANGEWOOD
Synopsis
by Christopher Golden

WHAT'S BEEN WRITTEN:

Strangewood is a fictional place created by TJ Randall—Thomas to all his readers—a wilder Hundred Acre Wood. Dragons and dwarves and scarecrows and hyena-boys and all manner of cute and cuddly, and dark and nasty, creatures call Strangewood their home. As a book series, it is the most popular thing to come along since Pooh himself. The movies and cartoons are on the way. Life should be perfect for Thomas Randall.

But it's not.

Thomas and Emily Randall are divorced. They have different households, not far from one another in Westchester County, and must share the time of their 5-year-old son, Nathan.

All in all, though, things could be worse.

And they will be.

The prologue to the novel *Strangewood* is an excerpt from what is apparently the "last" in the Strangewood children's series, *Fly Away to Strangewood*. It is clear from this excerpt, however, that this last book in the series was never finished.

Chapter one introduces us to Thomas Randall, who sits in a restaurant in Lower Manhattan and waits for his agent, Francesca, to arrive. He is in a bit of a hurry because he needs to pick Nathan up from school in Westchester by five o-clock.

Though Thomas doesn't know it, the world has changed around him.

When Francesca arrives, they begin talking business. Thomas is bothered by the fact that Strangewood seems less and less like his vision, his creation, and more like a product. Since the beginning, The Boy, the central character of Strangewood, has been Thomas. Now The Boy isn't him anymore. He doesn't know how to explain it, or what it means, but it bothers him.

Despite his reservations, however, Thomas has a family to think of, for he supports two households now. He makes a deal for a cartoon series, though he has doubts about its quality.

During the conversation, Thomas sees a man pass by outside the restaurant who looks and dresses exactly like Grumbler, a character from Strangewood. He rushes outside, incredulous. The man was a dwarf, and his appearance can be no coincidence. Here was someone purposely dressing like Grumbler, unless of course somebody was playing a trick on Thomas. It didn't matter, though, for the idea had already struck him after seeing this man that Strangewood could be done as a live-action film. Francesca is unnerved by the idea because she feels that certain elements in Strangewood would be too frightening in live-action.

Later, Thomas picks up Nathan from the afterschool program at the Catholic school he attends. Sister Margaret is there waiting, because Thomas is late. She voices concerns about the detrimental effects of the divorce on Nathan, and Thomas wonders if he and Emily shouldn't put their son back in counseling. He seems to be dealing fairly well, but it is difficult to tell.

On the way home, Nathan reveals to his father that his imaginary friend, "Crabapple," is afraid of Strangewood and all the characters in it. Crabapple has supposedly told Nathan that these characters want to kill him. Thomas sets his son straight on the fact that the characters of Strangewood aren't real.

After a wonderful father-son day together on Saturday, the evening brings nightmares for Nathan. If that's what they are. In the middle of the night the boy wakes up screaming, and Thomas runs into his room. For a moment, Thomas thinks he sees blood all over his son's sheets and thinks it belongs to the boy. Then he blinks, and it is gone. But Nathan insists that Crabapple has been murdered by Grumbler and Feathertop and some of the other characters from Strangewood, good and bad. Murdered because he was trying to protect Nathan.

Thomas does his best to calm his son, and barely notices as he returns to his room with Nathan that on the hall carpet there is a green feather. Feathertop is a pony with green feathers on his head.

Emily Randall is introduced in the midst of an inner conflict. She has recently become involved with a younger man named Joe Hayes. She might even be falling in love with him, but she is worried about how she is going to balance her role as mother and ex-wife with that of lover. It's going to be complicated, she knows.

Sunday morning, after eating his father's pancakes, Nathan goes out to play. Thomas gets a surprising call from Francesca, who convinces him to go to LA on Monday morning to meet with Fox to discuss the live-action Strangewood idea. As they finish their call, Thomas realizes Nathan is not in the back yard. Panicked, he runs outside to find a trail of odd clay-muddy footprints coming out of the woods behind the house. And Nathan is nowhere to be found!

Thomas hears laughter and rounds the side of the house to find Nathan following the muddy prints. Thomas is angry with the boy, mostly because he is afraid for him. But Nathan insists that the person who made the tracks is gone, and if he'd been there, Nathan would have called for his father, who he says is "the only person who could make him go away, anyway." Thomas has no idea what Nathan is talking about until he follows the tracks himself. They lead to the living room window, where bees swarm in a pattern on the glass. The pattern is a human face. The "mud" isn't mud at all. It's peanut butter, and smeared on the window is a peanut butter face imprint of the Peanut Butter General, one of the primary villains of Strangewood.

Thomas is furious, and a little scared. Some crackpot or stalker is playing tricks on him. But if it's a stalker, he doesn't want to put Nathan in danger.

Sunday night, Thomas brings Nathan home and Emily has cooked dinner for all of them. Afterwards, while Nathan is sent off to put on his pajamas and brush his teeth, Emily tells Thomas about her relationship with Joe. He knows he should be happy for her, but he can't help feeling angry and jealous. Meanwhile, he tells her about the incident with Crabapple the night before, and that he thinks Nathan should go back to counseling. They agree that the following weekend, Thomas will take Nathan away for the weekend, rather than keep him home.

When their argument over Emily's new relationship is over, Thomas goes to say goodnight to Nathan, but the boy isn't in his room. Thomas hears running water from the bathroom, and realizes Nathan must just be brushing his teeth. He goes in, and Nathan is there, standing on a little stool, staring into the mirror with toothbrush at the ready.

But he's not brushing. Foam dribbles down his chin, but the boy is frozen. Catatonic. Emily comes running at Thomas's exclamation, and soon the ambulance is on the way.

For the first time, we find ourselves in Strangewood. Nathan wakes in a wheelbarrow, being trundled down a dark and bumpy path by Bob Longtooth and Cragskull, two of the nasty villains of Strangewood. But these guys are nastier than they ever were in the books. Because this is for real. And Strangewood . . . well, Strangewood has been irrevocably altered. The Big Old Orchard is withered and black, the land is dead or dying. The Land of Bells and Whistles is blazing in a mighty conflagration.

Longtooth and Cragskull are bringing Nathan to their master, the dreaded Jackal Lantern. But it seems that all the rules have changed in Strangewood along with the landscape. For in the woods, the screams of the Orange Peelers can be heard, and Longtooth is afraid of the little savages. He doesn't think they're on anyone's side.

But he's wrong.

When Nathan attempts to escape, he is quickly and painfully brought down by his captors. But a moment later, who should appear but the Peanut Butter General himself, with the little, viscious Orange Peelers running around at his feet. The General, Nathan suddenly realizes, looks just like a picture of his Grandad (whom he never knew) in uniform, but covered with peanut butter and with bees buzzing around his head.

He seems to want to rescue Nathan. But the Peanut Butter General is a villain, isn't he?

Back in the real world, Thomas is in Nathan's hospital room while Emily is out using the phone. Suddenly, he smells the strong odor of oranges, and searches the room before realizing the smell is coming from Nathan. Then he hears flapping outside the window, and the implication is that it is Fiddlestick, a little dragon who is one of the lovable characters from Strangewood.

WHAT'S TO COME:

The novel will develop on both sides of the veil of reality. In Strangewood, Nathan is rescued by the Peanut Butter General and the Orange Peelers. However, over the course of the story, they are ambushed by Grumbler and Feathertop, who are working for the Jackal Lantern now. Nathan is then brought to the Jackal Lantern's lair, where he is held captive. All of this is a way to bring Thomas to Strangewood.

Meanwhile, in the real world, a great many things are happening. With Nathan in the hospital, the tension between Thomas and Emily continues to grow. When they should be drawing strength from one another, Emily's relationship with Joe is causing them to be hostile instead.

Thomas finally begins to receive more concrete messages and visitations from Strangewood, and eventually from major characters from the mythos in the flesh. He tries to tell Emily about this, but all she can see is a man becoming desperate and mad over the illness of his child. Thomas's life and business go to pot. His agent, Francesca, tries to get him to continue with business, but he seems to have abandoned any responsibility for his career. He's a mess.

Thomas explains to the dubious Emily that Strangewood isn't a fictional place, that it's real. As a child, he was in a horrible accident that left him comatose for several weeks. For that entire time, his spirit lived in Strangewood. That's why it was such a fully formed vision, why he wrote about it all this time.

Emily believes he had gone over the edge, and with Joe's support, she attempts to get legal custody of Nathan. Thomas, she says, is unstable. Emily will not be portrayed as a shrew in any way, however, but as a reasonable, loving woman and mother. After all, from her perspective, she's being perfectly reasonable.

Unfortunately, Thomas is not hallucinating. He is finally told by Laughing Boy and Fiddlestick that he should *not* go to Strangewood. That he should stay away no matter what. That Nathan's abduction is just an excuse to get him there and make him pay for what's happened to Strangewood. Somehow, it's all his fault.

Finally, overwhelmed by it all, Thomas determines to overdose, trying to be careful not to take enough pills to kill himself, but enough to leave him unconscious for as long as possible. It's a terrible risk, but he can do nothing else. Even if the Jackal Lantern is expecting him, Thomas must go. Nathan is his son, his only child, the most important thing in his life. If he must sacrifice his life, then so be it.

Back in the real world, Thomas's actions lead to Emily receiving custody of Nathan, and she wants to move him from the hospital. Thomas is in the same hospital, however, and the characters from Strangewood know that father and son must remain near one another if either is to have a chance of returning to the world. Thus, though she cannot see them as clearly, they try to make contact with Emily. She sees just enough to begin to doubt her own certainty of Thomas's madness. Though Joe thinks she's losing it, Emily allows her new doubt to prevail. She doesn't know what to believe, but another few days won't hurt.

In Strangewood, Thomas is horrified at what he finds. The devastation and corruption are almost total. Characters once trustworthy are now his bitter enemies, and those once evil are now his only hope. He is heartbroken by the twisted nature of this once fantastical place, but he knows the only thing that is important is finding Nathan.

Eventually, Thomas finds the wounded and dying Peanut Butter General, who really *is* the spirit of his father, Terence Randall. Thomas was not the first Randall to visit Strangewood, but he might be the last. Since his death, Terence has lived in Strangewood. When Thomas started writing about the place, and based the Peanut Butter General on his father, that's what Terence became. But he was never really a bad man. Thomas just wrote him that way.

But, the General tells him, when Thomas stopped believing in Strangewood, when he stopped using himself as the template for The Boy, the place started to go bad. When it stopped being about fun and imagination and started being just business, Strangewood was tainted. Thomas is crushed. He didn't mean for it to happen. He just grew up and took new responsibilities, did what any man must do for his family.

His father knows and agrees. The characters of Strangewood became too wrapped up in the fiction themselves, became too reliant on Thomas instead of on themselves. And now they want to punish him for it. But first, they want him to return things to the way they were. Which he can't. Together, Thomas, the injured Peanut Butter General, and several of the characters from Strangewood, set out on a trek across the fantasy land to meet the Jackal Lantern in battle and rescue Nathan.

Back in the real world, Thomas Randall is dying. Emily is at his bedside, and Joe is there to support her. She has seen even more, sees it even in his unconscious face. There's something real here, even if it's only in his mind. And Nathan's mind too. But something. She calls to both of them to come back to those who love them.

In the final battle, Nathan is rescued, of course. The Peanut Butter General is destroyed, but the Jackal Lantern is also defeated. As Nathan wakes, Thomas's life slips away in the real world, and in Strangewood, the peanut butter begins to cover his body. He becomes the Peanut Butter General, protector and hero of Strangewood. Together, he and the other characters will build the fantasy paradise again from scratch.

Joe and Emily are together at the funeral, and Emily crouches to hold a crying Nathan as his father's casket is lowered into the ground. But Nathan is going to be all right. Because he knows the difference between what's real and what's not real. And he knows that every night when he sleeps, he'll be running and playing in Strangewood with his father, and Laughing Boy, and Fiddlestick and all the others.

THE END

Christopher Golden is a novelist, journalist and comic book writer. His novels include the vampire epics *Of Saints and Shadows*; *Angel Souls & Devil Hearts* and *Of Masques and Martyrs*; the best-selling trilogy, *X-Men: Mutant Empire*, a series of *Buffy the Vampire Slayer* novels (which he co-wrote with Nancy Holder); *Hellboy: The Lost Army*; and the current hardcover *X-Men: Codename Wolverine*.

Golden's comic book work includes the Marvel Knights restart of *The Punisher*, as well as *Punisher/Wolverine: Revelation* and stints on *The Crow* and *Spiderman Unlimited*. Upcoming projects include several *Buffy the Vampire Slayer* specials and miniseries, a Wildstorm one-shot called *Night Tribes*, and *Batman: Real World*.

The editor of the Bram Stoker Award-winning book of criticism, *CUT!: Horror Writers on Horror Film*, he has written articles for *The Boston Herald*, *Disney Adventures* and *Billboard*, among others, and was a regular columnist for the worldwide service BPI Entertainment News Wire. He is one of the authors of *The Watcher's Guide: The Official Companion to Buffy the Vampire Slayer* and *Buffy the Vampire Slayer: The Yearbook*.

Before becoming a full-time writer, he was licensing manager for *Billboard* magazine in New York, where he worked on Fox Television's *Billboard Music Awards* and *American Top 40* radio, among many other projects.

Golden was born and raised in Massachusetts, where he still lives with his family. He graduated from Tufts University. His latest works include a new, original dark fantasy entitled *Strangewood*, which will be published in 1999 by Penguin Putnam, and a series of YA mysteries for Pocket Books, the first of which, *Body Bags*, will appear in mid-1999. Please visit him at www.christophergolden.com

W